RUTH
TRUSTING GOD

The Proclaim Commentary Series

THE PROCLAIM COMMENTARY SERIES

RUTH
TRUSTING GOD

OLD TESTAMENT
VOLUME 8

MATTHEW STEVEN BLACK

WENATCHEE, WASHINGTON

Ruth: Trusting God (The Proclaim Commentary Series)
Copyright © 2021 by Matthew Black
ISBN: 978-1-954858-25-1 (Print Book)
        978-1-954858-26-8 (eBook)

Proclaim Publishers
PO Box 2082, Wenatchee, WA 98807
proclaimpublishers.com

Cover art: *Ruth with Bundle of Grain from ShareFaith Media*

Unless otherwise quoted, Scripture quotations are from the ESV® Bible (The Holy Bible, English Standard Version®), copyright © 2001, 2016 by Crossway, a publishing ministry of Good News Publishers. Used by permission. All rights reserved.

Scripture quotations marked NASB are taken from the New American Standard Bible®, Copyright © 1960, 1962, 1963, 1968, 1971, 1972, 1973, 1975, 1977, 1995 by The Lockman Foundation. Used by permission.

Scripture quotations marked NKJV are taken from the New King James Version®. Copyright © 1982 by Thomas Nelson. Used by permission. All rights reserved.

Scripture quotations marked NIV are taken from The Holy Bible New International Version®, NIV® Copyright © 1973, 1978, 1984, 2011 by Biblica, Inc.® Used by permission. All rights reserved worldwide.

Scripture quotations marked CSB are taken from the Christian Standard Bible®, Used by permission. All rights reserved. CSB ©2017 Holman Bible Publishers.

Scripture quotations marked NLT are taken from the Holy Bible, New Living Translation, Copyright ©1996, 2004, 2007 by Tyndale House Foundation. Used by permission of Tyndale House Publishers, Inc., Carol Stream, Illinois 60188. All rights reserved.

Scripture quotations marked KJV are taken from the King James Version of the Bible.

All rights reserved. No part of this publication may be reproduced, stored in a retrieval system or transmitted in any form by any means, electronic, mechanical, photocopy, recording or otherwise, without the prior permission of the publisher, except as provided by USA copyright law.

Notes: (1) Ancient quotations have been at times changed to the ESV as well as some archaic language updated, and additional phrases added for clarification. At times verse references (non-existent until recent times) have been interspersed as well to guide the modern reader. (2) We have done our best to be careful in footnoting. Due to the nature of the sermonic material, various items are quoted freely, and may not have proper footnoting. If any great error is noticed, please contact the publisher, and it will be remedied in whatever way is available to us.

First Printing, December 2021, Manufactured in the United States of America

Dedicated to David and Yadi Mead. Your surrender to the Lord and his plans for you are breathtaking. All glory be to Christ!

CONTENTS

INTRODUCTION **13**
    Author and Date 14
    Message 14
    Testimony 16

1 | RUTH 1:1-18 TRUSTING GOD IN SUFFERING **17**
    Stop Running from God in Your Suffering (1:1-5) 18
        The Family 18
        The Famine 19
        The Funerals 22
    Start Running to God in Your Suffering (1:6-18) 25
        The Blessing of God 25
        Faith in God 25
        The Worship of God 28
        Applications 30

2 | RUTH 1:18-2:12 TRUSTING GOD TO USE ORDINARY PEOPLE **33**
    The People God Uses (1:19-22) 34
        God Uses Ordinary and Unlikely People 34
        God Uses Ordinary Activities 34
        God Uses Ordinary Places 35
        God Uses Ordinary People in Extraordinary Pain 35
        God Uses Ordinary Provision 37
    The Plan God Uses (2:1-9) 39
        A Man for God's Plan 39
        A Desire for God's Plan 40
        A Place for God's Plan 41
        Encountering God's Plan 41
    The Faith God Uses (2:10-13) 43
        A Sign of Faith 43
        A Testimony of Faith 44
        A Prayer of Faith 44
        A Confirmation of Faith 45

3 | RUTH 2:14-23 TRUSTING GOD WITH OUR BLESSINGS **47**
    Share Your Blessings (2:14-16) 49
        The Blessing of Servanthood 49
        The Blessing of Generosity 50

    The Blessing of Sharing 52
Praise God for Your Blessings (2:19-22) 52
    Praise God for Provision 52
    Praise God for Protection 55
Wait for God's Blessing in God's Time (2:23) 56
    Wait with Fellowship 56
    Wait with Faithfulness 56

4 | RUTH 3:1-18 TRUSTING GOD WITH NEW ENDEAVORS 59

Obedience in New Endeavors (3:1-5) 61
    Obedience Requires Humility 62
    Obedience Requires Action 64
    Obedience Requires Courage 65
    Obedience Requires Faith 66
Surprises in New Endeavors (3:6-9) 67
    Surprising Instructions 68
    A Surprising Reunion 68
    A Surprising Proposal 69
Wisdom in New Endeavors (3:10-14) 70
    The Wisdom of Prayer 70
    The Wisdom of Humility 71
    The Wisdom of Holiness 71
    The Wisdom of Modesty 72
Faith in New Endeavors (3:15-18) 73
    God's Past Faithfulness 73
    God's Present Faithfulness 74
    God's Future Faithfulness 74

5 | RUTH 4:1-12 TRUSTING GOD WITH OBSTACLES 77

Submit to Authority (4:1-6) 79
    The Priority of Authority 79
    The Providence of Authority 81
    The Plurality of Authority 82
    The Clarity of Authority 83
Check Your Motives (4:7-10) 85
    Motivated by Integrity 85
    Motivated by Responsibility 86
Seek God in Prayer (4:11-12) 87
    A Prayer for Legacy 87
    A Prayer for Consistency 88
    A Prayer for Offspring 88

6 | RUTH 4:13-22 TRUSTING GOD'S REDEEMER 91

The Marriage Points to Christ (4:13a) 91

- Jesus Became Our Near Kinsman 92
- Jesus Paid the Price for His Bride 93
- Jesus Completes the Work of Redemption 93

The Baby Points to Christ (4:13b-17) 94
- The Baby's Mother is Redeemed 94
- The Baby's Parents are Chaste 95
- The Baby's Birth is Miraculous 95
- The Baby's Legacy is Renowned 96
- The Baby's Influence is Multigenerational 97
- The Baby's Name Means "Worshipper" 97

The Genealogy Points to Christ (4:18-22) 98
- Christ's Family is Divinely Constituted 98
- Christ's Family is Diverse 99
- Christ's Family is Delivered 100

7 | IMAGES OF THE SPIRIT IN RUTH 103

- The Spirit and A Forever Family 104
- The Spirit and the Harvest 105
- The Spirit and Faith 106
- The Spirit and the Gentiles 107
- The Spirit and Inheritance 108
- The Spirit and the Bride 109
- The Spirit and the Baby 110
- The Spirit and Worship 110

ABBREVIATIONS

Common

cf – Latin "conferatur", compare, or see, or see also
ff – and following (pages or verses)
i.e. – Latin "id est", that is
e.g. – Latin "exempli gratia", for example

Books of the Bible

OLD TESTAMENT

Genesis	Gen	Esther	Est
Exodus	Exo	Job	Job
Leviticus	Lev	Psalms	Psa
Numbers	Num	Proverbs	Pro
Deuteronomy	Deut	Ecclesiastes	Ecc
Joshua	Josh	Song of Solomon	Song
Judges	Jdg	Isaiah	Isa
Ruth	Rth	Jeremiah	Jer
1 Samuel	1 Sam	Lamentations	Lam
2 Samuel	2 Sam	Ezekiel	Eze
1 Kings	1 Kgs	Daniel	Dan
2 Kings	2 Kgs	Hosea	Hos
1 Chronicles	1 Chr	Joel	Joel
2 Chronicles	2 Chr	Amos	Amos
Ezra	Ezr	Obadiah	Oba
Nehemiah	Neh	Jonah	Jonah

Micah	Mic	Haggai	Hag
Nahum	Nah	Zechariah	Zech
Habakkuk	Hab	Malachi	Mal
Zephaniah	Zeph		

New Testament

Matthew	Mt	Titus	Titus
Mark	Mk	Philemon	Phm
Luke	Lk	Hebrews	Heb
John	Jn	James	Jas
Acts	Acts	1 Peter	1 Pet
Romans	Rom	2 Peter	2 Pet
1 Corinthians	1 Cor	1 John	1 Jn
2 Corinthians	2 Cor	2 John	2 Jn
Galatians	Gal	3 John	3 Jn
Ephesians	Eph	Jude	Jud
Philippians	Phil	Revelation	Rev
Colossians	Col		
1 Thessalonians	1 Thess		
2 Thessalonians	2 Thess		
1 Timothy	1 Tim		
2 Timothy	2 Tim		

INTRODUCTION

Naomi took the child and laid him on her lap and became his nurse. And the women of the neighborhood gave him a name, saying, "A son has been born to Naomi." They named him Obed. He was the father of Jesse, the father of David.
RUTH 4:16-17

The events of the book happened sometime during the period of the Book of Judges (1375–1050 B.C.) according to Ruth 1:1. Judges 21:25 is the key to the historical setting of the book: "In those days Israel had no king, so the people did whatever seemed right in their own eyes."

The period of the judges was a time of political, religious, and moral chaos. The political chaos is seen in the cycles of apostasy that resulted in oppression by foreign powers. The religious chaos is seen in the person of Micah, who set up his own house priest instead of going to Shiloh to worship (Jdg 17). The moral chaos is illustrated in the perversions recorded in Judges 19. The book of Ruth must be seen in contrast with the book of Judges. The book of Ruth is an oasis of fidelity in a time of idolatry, sin, and infidelity.[1]

The Book of Ruth is read annually by orthodox Jews on the Feast of Pentecost. This feast commemorates the giving of the Law on Mount Sinai and occurs at the time of the beginning of the offering called the

---

[1] Robert B. Hughes and J. Carl Laney, *Tyndale Concise Bible Commentary*, The Tyndale Reference Library (Wheaton, IL: Tyndale House Publishers, 2001), 103.

Firstfruits of the Harvest (Exo 23:16). Ruth's betrothal took place during this festive harvest season, when barley was being winnowed (3:2; *cf* 1:22).[2]

AUTHOR AND DATE

No one knows for sure who wrote the Book of Ruth. Jewish tradition has attributed the book to Samuel. If he was the author, the book would have been written near the time when David was anointed king of Israel. One of the reasons, then, for Samuel's writing the Book of Ruth could have been to justify David's claim to the throne (through Ruth and Boaz, his great-grandparents). Since Ruth was the great-grandmother of David (Ruth 4:17), who began his rule at Hebron in 1010 b.c., the experiences in the Book of Ruth occurred in the last half of the 12th century. This means that Ruth may have been a contemporary of Gideon.[3]

MESSAGE

Ruth is a story within the unfolding story of the Bible. The way a Bible book starts and ends often gives important clues as to its main message. Ruth 1:1 sets it in a particular time in the history of God's people, Israel: "In the days when the judges ruled." The days of the judges were dark days. The last verse of Judges explains why: "In those days Israel had no king; everyone did what was right in their own eyes." If ever there was a recipe for disaster, that was it. The Book of Judges is a record of the chaos that occurs when people rebel against God and do their own thing.

One of the key words in Ruth is "kindness" (*cf* 1:8; 2:20) which points us to the overall theme of Ruth. God is kind and merciful to undeserving sinners. It is a translation of the Hebrew word *hesed*, meaning "loyal love." It is the covenant love the Lord had committed himself to showing to his people. And the story of Ruth is the outworking of the

---

[2] John W. Reed, "Ruth," in *The Bible Knowledge Commentary: An Exposition of the Scriptures*, ed. J. F. Walvoord and R. B. Zuck, vol. 1 (Wheaton, IL: Victor Books, 1985), 415.

[3] Ibid.

Lord's kindness, as he sets in place the line into which the king his people need would be born. This shows Ruth's place in the unfolding story of the whole Bible. The last five verses of Ruth are also found in Matthew 1:3–6 in the genealogy of our Lord Jesus Christ. The Lord Jesus is declared to be the Lord's chosen King, descended from King David (and therefore from Boaz and Ruth), who came as a result of the Lord's kindness to replace rebellious chaos with order.[4]

Ruth also stood in stark relief against the dark background of her own Moabite ancestry. Moses detailed the somber story of the nation of Moab's origin (Gen 19:30–38). Lot's two daughters despaired of any future after the destruction of Sodom and Gomorrah. In faithless irresponsibility they got their father drunk enough that he would have sex with them in the cave where they lived. The fruits of their incest were Moab and Ben-Ammi. These sons became the founders of the Moabites and the Ammonites, respectively, nations that often warred against Israel.

Ruth the Moabitess broke the tradition of her idolatrous people and her irresponsible ancestor, Lot's older daughter. Ruth became a believer in the God of the Hebrews. She sought her fulfillment as a mother through the gracious plan of the one true and living God. She proved herself to be worthy of being named with the finest women of Israel.

The grace of God was evident in that he included several non-Israelites in the line of David. Since this was the line through which Christ came, it foreshadowed God's inclusion of Gentiles in the work of David's greater Son, the Lord Jesus Christ. Four non-Israelite women are mentioned in Christ's genealogy in Matthew 1—Tamar (Mt 1:3), Rahab (Mt 1:5), Ruth (Mt 1:5), and Uriah's wife, who was Bathsheba (Mt 1:6). Tamar was a Canaanite, who became the mother of Judah's children, Perez and Zerah. Rahab was a Canaanite harlot in Jericho who became an ancestress of Boaz (*cf* Ruth 4:21). Ruth was a Moabitess who became the mother of Obed. Since Bathsheba, the mother of Solomon by David, had been the wife of Uriah, the Hittite, it was probable that she too was a Hittite.[5]

---

[4] Jonathan Prime, *Opening up Ruth*, Opening Up Commentary (Leominster: Day One Publications, 2007), 13–14.

[5] Reed, "Ruth," in *The Bible Knowledge Commentary*, 416.

TESTIMONY

The name Yahweh is used 17 times throughout the book of Ruth, and it emphasizes the relational aspect of faith. Ruth's God (and ours) is the covenant keeping God. He will never leave us nor forsake, even though we at times will leave him. Naomi and Elimelech left the promised land for a land of idolatry. Can a Christian come back to God if they have strayed? The answer is a resounding yes! We may try to leave God, but God will never leave us. No one can pluck us out of his hand. As the covenant keeping God, since he laid down the life of his Son for us, he will surely send goodness and mercy (*hesed*) after us all the days of our lives. His unrelenting love is chasing after you and me. The book of Ruth teaches us that we cannot outrun the love of God.

Matthew Steven Black
Elgin, Illinois
December 1, 2021

1 | RUTH 1:1-18
TRUSTING GOD IN SUFFERING

Where you go I will go, and where you lodge I will lodge. Your people shall be my people, and your God my God. Where you die I will die, and there will I be buried. May the LORD do so to me and more also if anything but death parts me from you.
RUTH 1:16-17

Pain is a constant in this life. You have either just finished a trial, are going through one right now, or are getting ready to go through one. These trials test our faith. Often, when we are going through a trial, it's hard to see what God is doing. We have a choice in the darkness and pain: pleasing God or pleasing self.

I remember when I got Jill's engagement ring. I got such a great deal on it I had to get it appraised. It was worth more than ten times what I paid for it. Trials and suffering and pain help us to appraise our faith. We find out where we are really at when we are tested. Bible knowledge is absolutely necessary, but it is not enough. We actually have to trust God, surrender to him, and depend on him to experience his eagle's wings carrying us. Trials grow and strengthen our faith. Ruth is a wonderful study of how the tangled web of our lives accomplish the greater and larger plan of God in the earth. Ruth is a study of God's love, his providence, and his plan for all who love and serve him, even in the tangled messes of our lives, our trials, and even our sins. God is greater than all our bad choices. We'll see that choosing God brings the greatest happiness to the human heart.

Ruth is the record of a Jewish family living in the terrible times of the Judges of Israel. During those years, "every man did that which was right in his own eyes" (Jdg 17:6; 21:25). In such a sin-filled setting, Ruth is a bright illustration of the grace of God and His abounding mercy. Grace is God's provision for man's need. It is His eternal and absolutely free favor, shown in salvation which he offers to all. The entire book of Ruth reveals the character and ways of God: His providence, sovereignty, grace, holiness, and His invitation of salvation to all people.

We do not deserve *anything* from God. He does not have to save us. Nor must he listen to us when we pray. He does not need to guide our lives, nor provide for our daily needs. But he does all this for us—and much, much more—because he is *gracious*. One purpose of the book of Ruth is to show that even in the Old Testament the grace of God included the Gentiles.

STOP RUNNING FROM GOD IN YOUR SUFFERING (1:1-5)

How should we deal with suffering? We are going to see the wrong way to deal with suffering – running from God (1:1-5). Then we'll see the godly way to deal with suffering – running to God (1:6-18). And as enter into the book of Ruth, remember it is during the time of Judges. This was a very dark and confused day. Ruth is living outside of Israel with her husband and two sons in Moab.

> **Ruth 1:1-2** | In the days when the judges ruled there was a famine in the land, and a man of Bethlehem in Judah went to sojourn in the country of Moab, he and his wife and his two sons. ² The name of the man was Elimelech and the name of his wife Naomi, and the names of his two sons were Mahlon and Chilion. They were Ephrathites from Bethlehem in Judah. They went into the country of Moab and remained there.

The Family

The names of people in the Bible tell a story. Naomi means "pleasantness" or we might say "sweetheart." Later on she's going to say call me Mara or "bitter pain" or "painful." Elimelech means "God is my King. Mahlon means "sick." Chilion means "dying."

The places assist us in understanding the story of Ruth. We read in verse 2, "They were Ephrathites from Bethlehem in Judah." Ruth doesn't know it, but she is marrying into royalty. Mahlon is an Ephrathite from Bethlehem. This would be like meeting someone from the UK and finding out you married someone from the "house of Tudor" from London, England. So Elimelech is royalty, but he doesn't know it. He doesn't know what God has in store for his family.

Ruth was born in the land of Moab. Moab was near the land of Israel. The Moabites and Israelites were enemies. Years before, God cursed the Moabites because they had been unfriendly to the people of Israel (when they were on their way from Egypt to Canaan–Deuteronomy 23:3-4). In Moab, Ruth's parents taught her about their gods–particularly the one called Chemosh (*cf* Num 21:29). She would have known that many human sacrifices had been offered to it (2 Kgs 3:26-27). You can imagine how this must have filled her with terror as a child.

Rabbis in the Talmudic tradition claimed that Ruth was likely the daughter of Eglon, king of the Moabites. Remember, he was the very fat king (*cf* Jdg 3:17) of Moab. God allowed King Eglon to conquer the Israelites because they had turned from worshiping Him. Quickly the rebellious people of Israel learned the awfulness of being ruled by a cruel king (Jdg 3:12-30). For 18 years the Moabites had ruled over the people of Israel. But when the Israelites truly repented of their rebellion and turned to God again, he forgave them. Then he helped a young Israelite man named Ehud to kill King Eglon of Moab. At last the people of Israel were free from the power of the Moabites. About that time, there was a famine in the land of Israel, and this is where the story of Ruth takes place.

The Famine

The Scriptures here do not expressly state it, but it leads us to wonder if the famine was not in fact God's judgment upon his people, because famine, if not every time, almost every time that it is mentioned in Scripture, is done so in conjunction with God's judgment against his people, because if they refuse to obey him, then he will refuse to feed them.

It is important to note in our day of plenty that food, that our daily food does not come from the grocer, but ultimately it comes from the Lord as a gift of grace. Bethlehem, literally means, "House of Bread."

But now God has stripped the House of Bread of its bread with this famine. How strange that there should be a famine in Bethlehem, this "house of bread"! In the Old Testament, a famine was often an evidence of God's discipline because His people had sinned against him (Lev 26:18–20; Deut 28:15, 23–24). During the time of the Judges, Israel repeatedly turned from God and worshiped the idols of the heathen nations around them; and God had to discipline them (Jdg 2:10–19). The godly had to suffer because of the ungodly, even in Bethlehem.[6] God's judgment seems to be on Israel, because 50 miles away the Moabites seem to be just fine. And the famine seems to only be surrounding God's people in Bethlehem.

And now we are intensely focused on this one family. There is a husband, his wife, their two boys: Mahlon and Chilion. The husband, Elimelech, is left with a decision to make, and that is, "Do I remain with my family in Bethlehem, where there is famine and people are literally starving to death? Or do I journey and relocate, move to Moab." Moab is some 50 miles away, and he decides he will go. So, we read in verse 2: "They went into the country of Moab and remained there."

In a good year there can be a good harvest in Israel, but in a bad year there can be insufficient rain at the right time, or a locust epidemic. The country is always only one step from famine. What is Elimelek to do? His own farm cannot feed his family, and presumably the famine affects everyone else in the area so they cannot simply bail him out. Somehow, he must provide for his family. Apparently other farmers in Bethlehem are just hoping to get by somehow. Perhaps they have been able to store up some grain from the good years and can now use it to get through the lean years, but evidently Elimelek has not been able to do that. He hears that things are better in Moab.[7] Based mainly on external factors, he moves to this neighboring pagan nation.

We ought not to criticize Elimelech. You've likely never been where he was. His sons were sick and dying, so he named them that. There is nothing that touches closer to home. What we are saying is not hat

---

[6] Warren W. Wiersbe, *Be Committed*, "Be" Commentary Series (Wheaton, IL: Victor Books, 1993), 13–14.

[7] John Goldingay, *Joshua, Judges, and Ruth for Everyone: A Theological Commentary on the Bible*, Old Testament for Everyone (Louisville, KY; London: Westminster John Knox Press; Society for Promoting Christian Knowledge, 2011), 163–164.

Elimelech was ungodly, but he was unwise. And so what he determines to do is not deal with the underlying spiritual causes of sin and rebellion and such. He instead – as many men do – simply looks at the economics and the job opportunity and the upward mobility that is afforded him in Moab, and he relocates his family to Moab, which at first glance does not seem like such a tragic, strategic error – because ultimately it is, because Moab is no place for God's people to dwell. The Bible tells us they didn't worship Yahweh, the God of Abraham, Isaac, and Jacob. They worshipped a false God named Chemosh. And so God's people weren't to move to Moab. God's people were not to dwell with Moabites.

So Elimelech serves as the tragic example of the man who did not count the spiritual costs of a relocation of his family. He didn't realize, or perhaps failed to rightly consider, that when a man makes decisions for his home and his family, he is perhaps mortgaging their future, thinking very shortsightedly. Where we live determines who our friends are, where or if we go to church, and often who our children marry.

When trouble comes to our lives, we can do one of three things: endure it, escape it, or enlist it. If we only endure our trials, then trials become our master, and we have a tendency to become hard and bitter. If we try to escape our trials, then we will probably miss the purposes God wants to achieve in our lives. But if we learn to enlist our trials, they will become our servants instead of our masters and work for us; and God will work all things together for our good and his glory (Rom 8:28).

Why Was Leaving Israel Wrong?

Elimelech made the wrong decision when he decided to leave home. What made this decision so wrong?

Elimelech sought safety through finances instead of by faith. Matthew 6:33, "But seek first the kingdom of God and his righteousness, and all these things will be added to you." The word of God expressly forbade God's people from settling in Moab.

Elimelech cared perhaps more for the physical than the spiritual. A husband and father certainly wants to provide for his wife and family, but he must not do it at the expense of losing the blessing of God. One of the devil's pet lies is: "You do have to live!" That was his temptation to our Lord. What was Jesus' answer? "Man shall not live by bread alone but by every word that proceeds out of the mouth of God." And it is *in God* that "we live and move and have our being" (Acts 17:28); and he is able to take care of us.

Elimelech seemed to trust the enemy more than the Lord. Elimelech's name we learned means, "God is my King." But he wasn't living like God was king. By going fifty miles to the neighboring land of Moab, Elimelech and his family abandoned God's land and God's people for the land and people of the enemy. The Moabites were descendants of Lot from his incestuous union with his firstborn daughter (Gen 19:30–38), and they were the Jews' enemies because of the way they had treated Israel during their pilgrim journey from Egypt to Canaan (Deut 23:3–6; Num 22–25). During the time of the Judges, Moab had invaded Israel and ruled over the people for eighteen years (Jdg 3:12–14); so why should Elimelech turn to them for help? They were a proud people (Isa 16:6) whom God disdained. "Moab is my washpot," said the Lord (Psa 60:8), a picture of a humiliated nation washing the feet of the conquering soldiers.

David's witness is worth considering: "I have been young, and now I am old; yet I have not seen the righteous forsaken, or his descendants begging bread" (Psa 37:25, NKJV). As Paul faced a threatening future, he testified, "But none of these things move me, neither count I my life dear unto myself" (Acts 20:24, KJV). In times of difficulty, if we die to self and put God's will first (Mt 6:33), we can be sure that he will either take us out of the trouble or bring us through.[8]

The Funerals

Suddenly we learn of some tragic news.

Naomi's Husband

Ruth 1:3 | But Elimelech, the husband of Naomi, died, and she was left with her two sons.

Why did Elimelech move to Moab? So that he wouldn't die. What did Elimelech do in Moab? He died. The truth is the safest place in the world is the center of God's will. It's hard to be content. It's hard to live in today's world. It's very much like Israel was back in Ruth's day.

---

[8] Wiersbe, *Be Committed*, 13-16.

There's a bit of hope in that. In that culture, they would look after her, care for her, feed her, nurture her in her old age. She would be okay because she had two sons. And that seems to be the case, at least at first.

The Widows

Ruth 1:4 | These took Moabite wives; the name of the one was Orpah and the name of the other Ruth. They lived there about ten years.

Naomi and Elimelech's sons are marrying girls who, in all likelihood, worship another god. Did that threaten to break Naomi's heart and impose on her a sense of failure and shame as a mother? What are nice Israelite boys doing marrying Moabite women? We all know about Moabite women. Think about where they came from (*cf* Gen 19:30–38).[9] These are Lot's children by incest. And they would be worshipping the child-sacrificing god Chemosh.

This is devastating, but in some ways, we must fault the father on two accounts. One, he moved them to Moab, so he only left the boys one option, that being marry a Moabite woman; and secondly, he apparently approved of these marriages. We as men need to realize that where we live is also where our sons and daughters will find their spouses. In the next verse, we see how God is in control, and even when we make bad choices, he can turn his providence to direct us in a new direction. And indeed, some more earth-shaking news is reported here.

Naomi's Sons

Ruth 1:5 | And both Mahlon and Chilion died, so that the woman was left without her two sons and her husband.

So now their husbands named "Sick" and "Dying" actually die. Why did Elimelech move to Moab? So that he and his wife and sons would not die. Now all but Naomi is dead, and Ruth and Orpah are childless. There is always a choice in suffering. What did Job do when he was faced with suffering?

Job 1:20-21 | Then Job arose and tore his robe and shaved his head and fell on the ground and worshiped. [21] And he said, "Naked I came from

---

[9] Goldingay, *Ruth for Everyone*, 164.

my mother's womb, and naked shall I return. The LORD gave, and the Lord has taken away; blessed be the name of the LORD."

What was Job's wife's response? Job 2:9, "Curse God and die." We can be like Adam and run and hide. Jonah also learned that you cannot run from God! Or we can be like Habakkuk 3 when he faced another famine. What was the Prophet Habakkuk's choice? His choice was to rejoice!

> *Habakkuk 3:17-18* | Though the fig tree should not blossom, nor fruit be on the vines, the produce of the olive fail and the fields yield no food, the flock be cut off from the fold and there be no herd in the stalls, [18] yet I will rejoice in the LORD; I will take joy in the God of my salvation."

What's the point? Bad things happen if, when suffering comes, we run away from God. Suffering is designed to draw us to God. C.S. Lewis said: "Pain is God's megaphone" to awaken us. There are so many sleepy Christians. God won't let his church sleep. J.C. Ryle said this:

> Affliction is one of God's medicines! By it he often teaches lessons which would be learned in no other way.... Health is a great blessing but sanctified disease is a greater. Prosperity and worldly comfort, are what all naturally desire, but losses and crosses are far better for us if they lead us to Christ. Let us beware of murmuring in the time of trouble. There are no lessons so useful as those learned in the school of affliction. There is no commentary that opens up the Bible so much as sickness and sorrow. The resurrection morning will prove that many of the losses of God's people were in reality, eternal gains. Thousands at the last day will testify with David, "It is good for me that I have been afflicted" (Psa 119:71).[10]

Who knows how God would have blessed Elimelech, had he remained in Bethlehem. We know it is never good to run from God-ordained trials.

---

[10] J. C. Ryle, *Expository Thoughts on John*, vol. 1 (New York: Robert Carter & Brothers, 1879), 253–254.

START RUNNING TO GOD IN YOUR SUFFERING (1:6-18)

The Blessing of God

God is ready to bless us as he did Naomi, but trials are there to enlarge our hearts so that our hearts might contain God's blessings without any ounce of pride.

Naomi's commitment to Yahweh is clear. Naomi says, "Yahweh has visited his people." She doesn't use Elohim when referring to God. She has told Ruth and Orpah about Yahweh. She uses the covenant name of God. She's committed.

> **Ruth 1:6** | Then she arose with her daughters-in-law to return from the country of Moab, for she had heard in the fields of Moab that the Lord had visited his people and given them food.

Wrong decisions were made, but Naomi responds to God's providence. God visited his faithful people in Bethlehem, but not his daughter in Moab. Naomi heard the report that the famine had ended; and when she heard the good news, she decided to return home. There is always "bread enough and to spare" when you are in the Father's will (Lk 15:17, KJV). How sad it is when people only hear about God's blessing, but never experience it, because they are not in the place where God can bless them.

So Naomi has a conversation with her two daughters-in-law about her soon departure for Israel. Fifty-four percent of the book is conversation. It's an unusual conversation, where we see a test of faith and a commitment of faith. We see how to respond to suffering.

In this conversation, Naomi, Ruth and Orpah are confronting some very bitter providences. God is not the author of sin, but all events pass through the hands of the Lord. He "works all things after the counsel of his own will" (Eph 1:11). He is sovereign and he is good. Do we believe this? In the following conversation we find three women. Two of them believe that God is good, and that he can be trusted in affliction. One, Orpah, perhaps has the outward shell of a believer, but eventually turns back to her false Moabite gods.

Faith in God

> **Ruth 1:7a** | So she set out from the place where she was.

It was time for Naomi to begin to walk by faith. How do you walk by faith? By claiming the promises of God and obeying the word of God, in spite of what you see, how you feel, or what may happen. It means committing yourself to the Lord and relying wholly on him to meet the need. When we live by faith, it glorifies God, witnesses to a lost world, and builds Christian character into our lives. God has ordained that "the righteous will live by his faith" (Hab 2:4; *cf* Rom 1:17).[11]

Naomi's Decision

Ruth 1:7 | So she set out from the place where she was with her two daughters-in-law, and they went on the way to return to the land of Judah

Hearing that there is abundant food in Bethlehem, Naomi determines to return to her homeland. Both her daughters-in-law begin the journey with her.

Naomi's Despair

Ruth 1:8-15 | But Naomi said to her two daughters-in-law, "Go, return each of you to her mother's house. May the Lord deal kindly with you, as you have dealt with the dead and with me. ⁹ The Lord grant that you may find rest, each of you in the house of her husband!" Then she kissed them, and they lifted up their voices and wept. ¹⁰ And they said to her, "No, we will return with you to your people." ¹¹ But Naomi said, "Turn back, my daughters; why will you go with me? Have I yet sons in my womb that they may become your husbands? ¹² Turn back, my daughters; go your way, for I am too old to have a husband. If I should say I have hope, even if I should have a husband this night and should bear sons, ¹³ would you therefore wait till they were grown? Would you therefore refrain from marrying? No, my daughters, for it is exceedingly bitter to me for your sake that the hand of the Lord has gone out against me." ¹⁴ Then they lifted up their voices and wept again. And Orpah kissed her mother-in-law, but Ruth clung to her. ¹⁵ And she said, "See, your sister-in-law has gone back to her people and to her gods; return after your sister-in-law."

---

[11] Wiersbe, *Be Committed*, 15–16.

As we read this conversation, it seems it is "anti-evangelism." Orpah is going to do what we would consider ordinary. She goes home. Ruth is going to do what is extraordinary, and she will refuse to go home. And in this we see that Orpah, when it really comes to an issue of faith and trust in God, she turns her back on God and returns home. We see that in verse 15. Naomi says to Ruth, after Orpah has left and gone home, "See your sister-in-law" – that is Orpah – "has gone back to her people and her gods." This is quite strange. This is anti-evangelism. But when we see it in context, this is a test of faith, and Orpah goes home because she looked like a believer but was faking it and really a pagan girl.

Naomi's Doctrine

We all have a doctrine of God. It's our theology. Naomi believed that God was sovereign in directing her life. Notice Naomi says something to the girls about God's providence in verse 13, "No, my daughters, for it is exceedingly bitter to me for your sake that the hand of the Lord has gone out against me." This is God's doing. God has a purpose in this. He is chastening me. Trials are scary, but what would be scarier would be a God who was not in control! God's purpose in affliction is sanctification. Listen to Spurgeon's comments.

> There is no attribute of God more comforting to his children than the doctrine of divine sovereignty. Under the most adverse circumstances, in the most severe troubles, they believe that sovereignty hath ordained their afflictions, that sovereignty overrules them, and that sovereignty will sanctify them all.[12]

In all her bitterness, Naomi had good doctrine. She recognized God's providential ordering of human life, specifically her life. We can see something Naomi couldn't: God's purpose for human history being fulfilled in David. Even in areas of possible sin in her or her husband's life, God accomplishes his overall plan. Ruth has to be rescued from Moab. What looks like a bad mistake of Naomi's son marrying a Moabitess, turns to the infinite mercy of God. Truly God can bring beauty from ashes. As we see Naomi, we behold God's hand upon her, and we can trace the mysterious outworking of God's overflowing goodness in

---

[12] Charles Spurgeon, "Divine Sovereignty" in *New Park Street Pulpit*, vol 2 (London: Passmore & Alabaster, 1856), 185.

her life. The events speak for themselves. In personal life and in history God was working out his good purpose.[13] He is doing the same for us!

The Worship of God

Ruth's statement in Ruth 1:16–18 is one of the most magnificent confessions found anywhere in Scripture. First, she confessed her love for Naomi and her desire to stay with her mother-in-law even unto death. Then she confessed her faith in the true and living God and her decision to worship Him alone. She was willing to forsake father and mother (2:11) in order to cleave to Naomi and the God of her people. Ruth was steadfastly "determined" to accompany Naomi (1:18) and live in Bethlehem with God's covenant people.

The Priority of God's People in Worship

> **Ruth 1:16-18** | But Ruth said, "Do not urge me to leave you or to return from following you. For where you go I will go, and where you lodge I will lodge. Your people shall be my people, and your God my God. **17** Where you die I will die, and there will I be buried. May the LORD do so to me and more also if anything but death parts me from you." **18** And when Naomi saw that she was determined to go with her, she said no more.

What's the issue? It's the worship of God at stake. Ruth says, "I'm not going home. There are no believers there. There's no church. You're the only believer in town. You left." Ruth desperately wants to go back to Israel with Naomi. Wherever Naomi goes is where Ruth is going! It's a worship issue. She can't go back to the Moabites because she's now a believer in Yahweh. She's determined to live in Israel. But there was a divine law that forbid her from worship at the tabernacle.

> *Deuteronomy 23:3* | An Ammonite or Moabite shall not enter the congregation of the Lord; even to the tenth generation none of his descendants shall enter the congregation of the Lord forever" (NKJV).

This meant permanent exclusion. How then could Ruth enter into the congregation of the Lord? By trusting God's grace and throwing herself completely on his mercy. Law excludes us from God's family,

---

[13] Joyce G. Baldwin, "Ruth," in *New Bible Commentary: 21st Century Edition*, ed. D. A. Carson et al., 4th ed. (Leicester, England; Downers Grove, IL: Inter-Varsity Press, 1994), 288.

but grace includes us if we put our faith in Christ.[14] In God's perfect plan, though she would have been forbidden from entering the tabernacle, she would bear the child that is Lord not only over the tabernacle and temple, but of the entire universe.

Despite her being an outsider and excluded from corporate worship, Ruth the Moabitess has an amazing faith. She understood that God's special place is not a tabernacle made with hands, but the hearts of his people. She was at home with those who loved Yahweh just as she did. She was willing to make great sacrifice to congregate with God's people. Consider this: she is going back to Israel with no husband, no home, no friends, no family, no job, no food. She may have greater faith than Abraham. If you remember the story of Abraham, he left his hometown and his family and their religion of worship of a false god to go somewhere else and start over with Yahweh. Why did he do that? Because God told him to. Ruth's story is in many regards similar to Abraham's. She left her family, her hometown, and her religion to go start a new life in a new town with Yahweh, with one notable distinction, that being God never spoke to her. God never told Ruth to go. She was determined to prioritize God's people.

The Priority of Conversion in Worship

Ruth had come to trust in the God of Israel (2:12). She was born again, and she saw things differently than anyone in Moab. She was now "seeking first" the God of Israel. She had experienced trials and disappointments, but instead of blaming God, she had trusted him and was not ashamed to confess her faith. In spite of the bad example of her disobedient in-laws Ruth had come to know the true and living God; and she wanted to be with His people and dwell in his land.

Ruth's conversion is evidence of the sovereign grace of God, for the only way sinners can be saved is by grace (Eph 2:8–10). Everything within her and around her presented obstacles to her faith, and yet she trusted the God of Israel.[15]

When we are converted and we have made God's people our priority, we can face anything. And the opposite is also true. If we isolate ourselves, we will fall apart rather quickly. We need our fellowship with

---

[14] Wiersbe, *Be Committed*, 21–22.
[15] Ibid.

God and we need our fellowship with other Christians. When that is in place we can face any suffering that God brings our way.

Applications

So how are we to deal with suffering? God is good and God is sovereign.

Holiness for Christ

Ruth had to separate herself from her own people and join God's "forever family." Ruth is a beautiful picture of what is coming in the new covenant through Jesus. In Jesus, God removes all the hostilities of the flesh: race, history, hatred, war, etc. We are made one in Christ.

> *Ephesians 2:14* | He [Jesus[himself is our peace, who has made us both one and has broken down in his flesh the dividing wall of hostility.

Ruth had to leave Moab, but she was gaining a new family in Yahweh. This would be a forever family for her.

Conformity to Christ

Remember God's purpose in your suffering is conformity to Christ. God does not bring pain, but only to bring us closer to himself. Robert Murray McCheyne said,

> God's children should not doubt his love when he afflicts. Christ loved Lazarus peculiarly, and yet he afflicted him very sore. A surgeon never bends his eye so tenderly upon his patient, as when he is putting in the lancet, or probing the wound to the very bottom. And so with Christ – he bends His eye most tenderly over His own at the time He is afflicting them... A goldsmith when he casts gold into the furnace looks after it.[16]

God is good to prune us. He is good to cut us down to make us more like Christ, and to make us more fruitful.

> *John 15:1–2* | I am the true vine, and my Father is the vinedresser. ² Every branch in me that does not bear fruit he takes away, and every branch that does bear fruit he prunes, that it may bear more fruit.

---

[16] Robert Murray McCheyne. *Comfort in Sorrow* (Fearn, UK: Christian Focus, 2002), 11.

Remember that David wrote about half of the Psalms, most of them when he was hiding in caves from Saul or on the run from his son Absalom. When was David in the worst place? Not in the cave but when he was in his comfort zone. It was in his comfort zone that he fell with Bathsheba. So much good came out of him when he was in the caves.

Ruth doesn't know what God has in store for her. She has suffered so much, but she knows God is good and that he is great and sovereign.

Fruitfulness for Christ

Jonathan Edwards was one of the godliest men we can think of. Yet he was kicked out of his church for taking a stand for regeneration (against the halfway covenant) and he died from a vaccination at the tender age of 55 before he would become the president of Princeton College (now University). Sarah Edwards reflected on God's bitter providence on hearing that her husband died:

> What shall I say? A holy and good God has covered us with a dark cloud. O that we may kiss the rod and lay our hands on our mouths! The Lord has done it. He has made me adore his goodness, that we had him [her husband] so long. But my God lives; and he has my heart. O what a legacy my husband, and your father, has left us! We are all given to God; and there I am, and love to be.[17]

No one could have known how God would use Jonathan Edwards in an even greater way. He didn't need him to be president of Princeton. He wanted to use his writings.

Charles Haddon Spurgeon sums up the first chapter of Ruth very well: "Those who dive in the sea of affliction bring up rare pearls."[18] God has some things he wants to do through you, but he has to crush you to get you ready. This is God's way. Think of Moses, cast out of Egypt at 40 and then 40 years in the wilderness. But then came the burning bush. Think of Joseph, thrown away into a pit, and then into slavery in Potiphar's house, and then into a prison. It was only after he suffered that he was ready for a palace.

---

[17] Iain Murray, *Jonathan Edwards: A New Biography* (Carlisle, PA: Banner of Truth, 2002), 442.

[18] Charles Spurgeon, "The Golden Key of Prayer" in *Metropolitan Tabernacle Pulpit*, vol 11 (London: Passmore & Alabaster, 1865), 145.

Conclusion

Naomi and Ruth left Moab. They didn't have anything but the Lord, and we are going to see that that would be more than enough. Knowing Christ is sufficient for all the wisdom we will need for all the choices we are called on to make (Pro 9:10; *cf* 2 Pet 1:3). May the Lord help us to trust in the Lord during times of suffering and rest in the words of the Psalmist in Psalm 119.

> *Psalm 119:71* | It is good for me that I was afflicted, that I might learn your statutes.

We can trust God in our suffering. If we dive deep into the sea of affliction, let us look for God's pearls! We need to run to him, not away from him. We know this story well. These difficult decisions of faith will result in Ruth marrying Boaz and having a son that is in the direct line of Jesus Christ. God uses suffering in our lives to guide us into his will. Don't resist God but run to him in your pain.

2 | RUTH 1:18-2:12
TRUSTING GOD TO USE ORDINARY PEOPLE

> *The women said, "Is this Naomi?" She said to them, "Do not call me Naomi; call me Mara, for the Almighty has dealt very bitterly with me. I went away full, and the LORD has brought me back empty. Why call me Naomi, when the LORD has testified against me?"*
> RUTH 1:19-21

Ruth is in many ways a wonderful shadow of the gospel of Jesus Christ. Here we have this unworthy Moabite woman– a Gentile, a foreigner, completely out of place and unworthy, who we will find is rescued by Boaz and brought into favor forever by becoming the great grandmother of King David, and the ancestor of our Lord Jesus Christ.

In our text, Ruth is going to arrive in Bethlehem with Naomi and meet Boaz. She has absolutely nothing. Yet in God's economy, that's not a bad situation. When you have absolutely nothing, when you are at rock bottom, that is when God works the best. This is when he loves to work, because remember, "God resists the proud, but gives grace to the humble" (1 Pet 5:5). It is when we have nothing that we are most ready to receive the blessing of God.

As we consider that God uses ordinary people, we are going to see three things about how God wants to use us. It is a surprise that God wants to use us (1:19-22). It is in the sovereignty of God that we are used (2:1-9). We also see the goodness of God when he uses us (2:10-13).

THE PEOPLE GOD USES (1:19-22)

We read about the unlikelihood of God using Ruth and Naomi. So in Ruth 1:19, the story focuses on Naomi, and really, the book of Ruth is actually the story of Naomi. How can God bless an old barren widow? How can God use a woman who has absolutely nothing? It's a surprising thing that God uses any one of us.

God Uses Ordinary and Unlikely People

You may be asking: can God use me? Perhaps you have had the absolutely worst circumstances that could happen. You've made the most horrendous choices. I'm here to tell you that God can us *anybody*. And if you don't speak up for him in your life, he can make the rocks cry out!

Ruth and Naomi make their way back on the fifty-mile journey to Bethlehem, the House of Bread. Who could have known that on a human level, the centerpiece of redemptive history at this time was a Moabite woman? No one would ever imagine God would use someone the former idol worshipper, now dedicated follower of the Lord. On to Bethlehem she and Naomi trekked.

God Uses Ordinary Activities

> **Ruth 1:19a** | So the two of them went on until they came to Bethlehem.

Naomi and Ruth began their journey walking to Bethlehem. Walking is such an ordinary activity, but God can use those simple activities to conform us to Christ. We can imagine the fellowship they had on this journey. We don't know what they said to each other on their journey, but from what is revealed in the rest of the book, they must have had much fellowship and spoken about the Lord. Naomi knew Deuteronomy 6.

> *Deuteronomy 6:6-7* | These words that I command you today shall be on your heart. ⁷You shall teach them diligently to your children, and shall talk of them when you sit in your house, and when you walk by the way, and when you lie down, and when you rise.

Naomi probably used that 50-mile journey as an opportunity to continue to mentor and disciple her "daughter" Ruth. The everyday duties of life become a classroom for God's people.

It seemed like a simple journey to Bethlehem, but it was one that would change the history of the world. Extraordinary things happen when you give ordinary moments to God. Naomi likely used those moments like she had used all the other ordinary moments in her life. She served and loved God. She seemed to always obey and love God. She served others. She was one, it is apparent, that was always talking, instructing about God, praying for others, always using ordinary moments to build the faith of her greatest mission field, which was her family. Naomi was a great missionary mom.

God Uses Ordinary Places

Bethlehem was a tiny town. We sing about it today: "O little town of Bethlehem." But it is here that God begins his breakthroughs in the life of Naomi and Ruth.

> **Ruth 1:19b** | So the two of them went on until they came to Bethlehem. And when they came to Bethlehem, the whole town was stirred because of them.

Naomi arrived in town, and it was like Naomi was the first story of the evening news! It was like she was on every blog – everybody had an opinion. "Naomi's back in Bethlehem!" There was a lot to talk about! "You've been gone so long! Your husband and sons died! Who is this Moabite girl?" It is in this little town, whether people understand it or not, that God is going to set the stage for redemptive history.

It was God's will that Naomi return to this little town of Bethlehem. She made a hard decision. She knew there might be reproach and people might not understand. But she made the hard choice to follow the Lord. She was a woman who served the Lord with seriousness and zeal. That brought her to this ordinary tiny village that seemed like it would be forgotten, but when God is in the mix, he can take the ordinary and make it extraordinary.

God Uses Ordinary People in Extraordinary Pain

It's clear that Naomi is utterly broken. Her husband is gone. He sons are gone. Yet sadly death touches everyone on planet earth. Naomi's circumstances were earth shattering for her, but so are they for the vast majority of the human race. Sadly, catastrophic circumstances are the norm on this planet. And God can use brokenness.

The Pain of Lost Reputation

After having faithfully served the Lord, it seems as if the Lord has not blessed her. She serves the Lord, and yet her reputation is torn to shreds. She serves the Lord with zeal, and things get even worse. She keeps serving the Lord, and things if they can, get even worse. It seems that the more faithful Naomi is, the more bitter her life becomes. So Naomi comes to town and changes her name. Can God use Naomi? Naomi does not think so.

> **Ruth 1:19c-20** | And the women said, "Is this Naomi?" [20] She said to them, "Do not call me Naomi; call me Mara, for the Almighty has dealt very bitterly with me.

We make a mistake when we think that God using us means that he makes our life a bed of roses. You see, God has never promised us that life would be easy. In fact life is a lot like a tapestry. Looking at our life is like peering underneath a loom, just loose ends of twine and string and yarn and knots of free will and choice, and it just looks like a mess. All Naomi saw was heartache. All she saw was death and devastation and famine. All she saw was the lonely mat she slept on each night. Yet from above the loom, from God's perspective it's this glorious tapestry as he's weaving together all of the details of our life.

God can take brokenness and turn it into something beautiful. He can restore the years that the locusts have eaten. You see God was using Naomi in the mess! God can turn a mess into a masterpiece.

> *Isaiah 55:8-9* | For my thoughts are not your thoughts, neither are your ways my ways, declares the LORD. [9] For as the heavens are higher than the earth, so are my ways higher than your ways and my thoughts than your thoughts.

Don't you know that God is the Master of the mess? And our mess is God's masterpiece (Eph 2:10). From the bottom of the tapestry, all we see are tangled knots and disordered colors, but from the top, there is a masterpiece that reflects the goodness and kindness of God. Yet all Naomi saw was the mess. So she asks why?

The Pain of Lost Perspective

Ruth 1:21 | I went away full, and the LORD has brought me back empty. Why call me Naomi, when the LORD has testified against me and the Almighty has brought calamity upon me?

Naomi can't see God because of all her pain. She doesn't feel God's love, but God harshness. Naomi says, "Don't call me sweetheart, call me bitter old woman." Call me "wounded." "Just let me die. I'll never recover. What can I do for God?" What Naomi couldn't see was the tapestry God was weaving on the other side. Who is Naomi? Through Ruth, she's the great, great grandmother of the greatest king of Israel – King David.

Naomi's theology is right. Amos 3:6 says, "Does calamity come to a city, unless the Lord has done it?" Calamity shakes things up in our lives. Do not be surprised by it. God often uses extreme and difficult circumstances to bring about his sovereign plan. Sometimes he's chiseling you. Sometimes he's using you to reach others. All the time God is good and sovereign. Those are the ingredients of providence.

Was Naomi feeling the bitter effects of life? There's not circumstances much more extreme than Naomi. Naomi is the female Job of the Old Testament! And this is the amazing thing, Naomi had the bitterest life anyone can imagine. But did Naomi stop being faithful when life got bitter? No! That's the point.

Naomi is not in sin. Sometimes life is bitter. She's not mad at God. She's wounded, torn up, and broken. And that's ok. God often has to till the ground and break our hearts before he plants the seed and grows the garden. Psalm 51:17, "The sacrifices of God are a broken spirit; a broken and contrite heart, O God, you will not despise." Naomi was saying: "Life is bitter. I am broken!" And that's ok. Naomi is the godliest woman in the book of Ruth. Ruth learned all that she knew about the Lord from the godly Naomi.

God Uses Ordinary Provision

We get a little foreshadowing as Naomi and Ruth return to Israel. It's clear upon their return that people are readying themselves for the harvest. This is the springtime, the feast of Pentecost. This is the time of life and fruitfulness and the joy of harvest. Is Naomi and Ruth going to starve? Never, not among God's people. Even in this dark time of the judges, the people follow at least some of the laws of Moses, which means there is enough barley to go around.

> **Ruth 1:22** | So Naomi returned, and Ruth the Moabite her daughter-in-law with her, who returned from the country of Moab. And they came to Bethlehem at the beginning of barley harvest.

Sometimes we wrongly look at our relationship the Lord as a barter system. I obey, and God pays my bills. Perhaps Naomi was confused that perhaps God had forgotten to bless her despite her obedience and faith. I mean after all, she pointed Ruth to know the Lord.

What was Naomi's job? To follow the Lord, follow her husband. Did she do those things? Yes! What else was Naomi's job? To live for the Lord, to shine her light. Did she do that? Absolutely! Her job was to bring a Moabite named Ruth to faith in Yahweh. She didn't know that was her job, but that was God's job for her. Even in all her bitter circumstances, Naomi chose to serve the Lord. And God bore fruit through her.

Naomi's goal in life was not simply to live a posh life. Her goal was to be faithful to the Lord. But what Naomi was learning is that God doesn't owe us a posh life. Naomi was learning in unbarable pain that the chief end of man is not a comfortable life, but to enjoy God now and forever. I like Naomi, because Naomi is a lot like you and me! Sometimes I am confounded. Sometimes I am confused. I can hardly see God in the pain of life. Sometimes life is bitter. She says, "Don't call me sweetheart, call me bitter old woman." I'm wounded. I'm torn up. God is sovereign. He doesn't do what we want him to do. He confounds us at times. Sometimes he gives us very bitter circumstances in life. It's not because God is forgetful or cruel. No God is doing something great in our lives.

A Provision of New Souls

As we look to the harvest with Naomi, she's going to go from bitterness to blessing fairly quickly. In fact, she's already fruitful for the Lord. She's led her daughter-in-law Ruth to faith in the Lord. So the harvest points us to this provision and harvest of souls. Ruth doesn't come to Bethlehem without Naomi's evangelism. God uses us in ways that we often cannot see. If we could see them, we might become proud.

Do you know who reached Charles Haddon Spurgeon for Christ? He tells the story of his conversion, that one wintery day he could not make it to church because of the blizzard. So he went to a tiny Methodist church. The pastor wasn't there because of the weather, so a deacon preached from Isaiah 45:22, "Look unto me, and be ye saved, all the ends of the earth: for I am God, and there is none else." We don't know who that deacon was, but God used that snowstorm so he could give that simple message to a 15-year-old boy who would turn the world upside down!

A Provision of a New Season

As Naomi and Ruth look around Bethlehem, it's clear that it's about time to harvest the fields. Naomi and Ruth just happened to be there at barley harvest. Barley harvest? What is that? That, dear saints, is hope. The famine is gone. God's providential hand of kindness and *hesed* blessing has arrived. It's a whole new season in Israel. Maybe it's a whole new season in the life of Naomi and Ruth. We have to continue, by faith, to see what God might do.

So we have a ton of imagery here. Naomi and Ruth are barren widows with no hope, but Bethlehem is pregnant with barley and fruit and harvest! This is a picture of God's blessing on them. They may be barren, but they are now pregnant with God's blessing on them. What a surprise!

THE PLAN GOD USES (2:1-9)

One of the biggest things single people want to know is, what is God's plan for my love life? When I was younger there used to be various dating shows on television. There would be a bachelorette who would choose someone to date. They would ask questions to see which one was the most suitable suitor. I'm glad that in God's plan, he promises to guide our steps for the best circumstances to conform us to Christlikeness. We see that God sovereignly directs our steps in all things. It's sometimes surprising how God directs circumstances, but it is always fascinating to see how it all works out.

A Man for God's Plan

> **Ruth 2:1** | Now Naomi had a relative of her husband's, a worthy man of the clan of Elimelech, whose name was Boaz.

God has a man lined up for his plan. Here we are introduced to Boaz is a worthy man – that's what his name means. He's worthy of respect. He's worthy of trust. He's worthy of imitation. Yes, he's worthy, but he's less than ordinary. His mother, do you remember her? Her name is Rahab, named after an Ammonite God. She's a Canaanite from Jericho. Her name means "Fierceness." She was fierce in the world when she was lost. And she became fierce for the Lord. She was on fire. She married Salmon – who was a leader in Israel. But here is a half Canaanite living among the Israelites. So he's rich. He's worthy, but he's single!

Now, furthermore, when it says that he's a worthy man, that phraseology, used elsewhere in the Old Testament, sometimes refers to a man of war – so he could fight. He's a man of war, a man of wealth, and a man who is worthy and godly. He's got everything going for him, but he's single. He's a Canaanite. Perhaps there's some racism going on in Israel.

A Desire for God's Plan

Ruth has a plan, and it's interesting. God uses Ruth's good and godly desires to carry out his own sovereign plan. Ruth's plans fit within the plans he has for her. God made marriage, and as long as we are seeking someone following the Lord, our desires are good. Ruth's desires are good and blessed by God.

> **Ruth 2:2** | And Ruth the Moabite said to Naomi, "Let me go to the field and glean among the ears of grain after him in whose sight I shall find favor." And she said to her, "Go, my daughter."

Here goes Ruth to the field to help provide for her mother-in-law. She's got no money, no real job. She's kind of on welfare. Gleaning is the equivalent to social services, food bank, homeless shelter, soup kitchen, food stamps. That's the Hebrew equivalent. And the way it works is this. God, in the Old Testament, he told his people, "The land belongs to me. So if you own a piece of land, actually I own it, too, and when you work the land, harvest what I give you for food, but don't take all of the food. Leave a little bit so that the poor, the widow, the orphan, the alien, the oppressed, the immigrant, the needy, can work" – not just get a handout, but work – "come to the field, and take some of the food home for themselves and their family." This was the Hebrew welfare system.

Naomi and Ruth have hit rock bottom. The equivalent would be one of you young ladies, moving to Chicago, only knowing one person, and being flat broke, out collecting aluminum cans to scrounge together a few bucks, sleeping at the mission, eating at the soup kitchen, I mean, these are women who are in a devastated, very difficult place.

A Place for God's Plan

> **Ruth 2:3** | So she set out and went and gleaned in the field after the reapers, and she happened to come to the part of the field belonging to Boaz, who was of the clan of Elimelech.

God has a place where his plan's going to take place. It all begins in a field. We learn that Ruth just "happened to come to the part of the field belonging to Boaz." You might wonder, "Why does the Bible say it that way?" It says it in an ironic way to get our attention. This isn't happenstance, circumstance, fortune, chance.

Here comes Boaz, stepping out of the Escalade, coming to check out his field, to see how things are going at the business. A very important man, a very rich man, a very successful man. And Ruth "happened" to choose that field.

There is no Murphy's Law for the child of God. Everything that can go wrong will go wrong. That's not true for the Christian. Everything that can go wrong might, but it will be made beautiful in God's time.

Encountering God's Plan

So often, we want something, and that's not bad. The only thing God requires is that we submit it to him. He gets to make the ultimate decision whether or not that thing we desire is best for his ultimate plan to conform us to Christ. We can't hold on to things to tightly. But we see here that as Ruth goes forward with her desires, God blesses her plans, and we see their first encounter. They don't meet here, but Boaz notices her. It begins with Boaz greeting the reapers.

> **Ruth 2:4** | And behold, Boaz came from Bethlehem. And he said to the reapers, "The LORD be with you!" And they answered, "The LORD bless you."

This is not most people's employer. Boaz is a godly man. He knows the Lord. He wants his employees to know the Lord. He greets them with a short form of the Levitical blessing.

Leviticus 6:24-26 | The LORD bless you and keep you; ²⁵ the LORD make his face to shine upon you and be gracious to you; ²⁶ the LORD lift up his countenance upon you and give you peace.

In the time of the judges, when everyone did that which was right in their own eyes, Boaz was a man of faith who lived in the presence of God. The fear of the Lord gave him incredible wisdom, and his financial situation was blessed.

Seeking God's Will

Boaz is extremely eligible. But he's half Canaanite. What girl would want him? He's got his eye on this new girl from Moab. So he enquires after her. Who is she? Does she know the Lord? Nothing is more important in dating and marriage than whether or not the person knows the Lord. So Boaz inquires. He's seeking God's will.

> **Ruth 2:5** | Then Boaz said to his young man who was in charge of the reapers, "Whose young woman is this?"

"Who is this girl?" Boaz inquires. She's gathering food from Boaz's field, like his "soup kitchen." She's poor. She's all dirty with no makeup just working hard. What does Boaz notice? I'm sure he saw her beauty. But what he noticed was her character! A servant tells him all about what a godly girl and hard worker she is.

> **Ruth 2:6-7** | And the servant who was in charge of the reapers answered, "She is the young Moabite woman, who came back with Naomi from the country of Moab. ⁷ She said, 'Please let me glean and gather among the sheaves after the reapers.' So she came, and she has continued from early morning until now, except for a short rest."

Boaz notices Ruth. She didn't have time to do her makeup. She didn't say, "Why didn't you call?" Some of us need four hours to get all ready. This is one of the greatest encounters of the Old Testament, and Ruth is without makeup. Ladies, you don't need make up. In the Hebrew Bible, you know what's after Proverbs? The book of Ruth. Proverbs closes with what great wisdom? The Proverbs 31 woman. Who is the Proverbs 31 woman – Ruth is!

> *Proverbs 31:30* | Charm is deceitful, and beauty is passing, but a woman who fears the LORD, she shall be praised."

But there is Ruth in the field. It says she got there at sun up, and she's been tirelessly working all day. Boaz is impressed.

Trusting God's Will

It seems Boaz is interested in Ruth, but he's not forward. He is a gentleman. He wants to make sure she is taken care of. He is not in any hurry. He's walking in step with the Lord. We see that in his gentle spirit as he provides for and protects this Moabite beauty.

> **Ruth 2:8-9** | Then Boaz said to Ruth, "Now, listen, my daughter, do not go to glean in another field or leave this one, but keep close to my young women. ⁹ Let your eyes be on the field that they are reaping, and go after them. Have I not charged the young men not to touch you? And when you are thirsty, go to the vessels and drink what the young men have drawn."

So Boaz doesn't know this is going to be his wife. He has an ethic. He loves Jesus. He has a job.

"Keep close to Ruth." He tells the women. He gives Ruth companionship with other godly women.

"Have I not charged the young men not to touch you?" he says. He had the right view of women. Women were not an object to Boaz.

He says to the young men – "Hey if you touch her, you see that field over there – we'll take care of you! Not really, but you know Boaz was Old Testament. Regardless, those who love God will protect women. Boaz was that kind of man. Ladies, if a man is interested in you, you need to ask him if he has a job and if he loves Jesus. In that order. He needs to be a man of character and a man of provision.

THE FAITH GOD USES (2:10-13)

Ruth and Boaz both show a great amount of faith and trust in God as they meet each other. What a lesson of trust for us in dating and courtship as well as in all of life.

A Sign of Faith

As Ruth encounters Boaz for their first face to face meeting, she bows to the ground, showing great meekness and humility.

> **Ruth 2:10** | Then she fell on her face, bowing to the ground, and said to him, "Why have I found favor in your eyes, that you should take notice of me, since I am a foreigner?"

Ruth falls on her face which was an appropriate custom in the Hebrew culture in the presence of an authority. It was a proper sign of respect. She's not forward. She's waiting on God. She simply asked him a question. She wanted to know his motives. Ladies, be careful not to give your heart to a man. You must know that he loves Jesus and that he has intentions for you.

A Testimony of Faith

Before Boaz ever meets her, he had seen and heard of her faith and godly testimony in the community of Bethlehem.

> **Ruth 2:11** | But Boaz answered her, "All that you have done for your mother-in-law since the death of your husband has been fully told to me, and how you left your father and mother and your native land and came to a people that you did not know before."

Ruth was a woman of character. Ruth is the Proverbs 31 woman. This is the first encounter between Ruth and Boaz, and Ruth's not all dolled up. She's grimy, sweaty, and without any makeup. Boaz notices Ruth's character.

Listen, if you are single, you will not find the right person if God is not first in your heart. Jesus Christ and his kingdom must be first in your heart before you seek to give your heart to another.

A Prayer of Faith

Now what does Boaz do? Ask for her phone number? Make a pass at her? Absolutely not. He prays for her outloud.

> **Ruth 2:12** | "The Lord repay you for what you have done, and a full reward be given you by the Lord, the God of Israel, under whose wings you have come to take refuge!"

Boaz prays and then he answers the prayer he prays. God wants us to not simply pray but be willing to be the vessel God will fill to answer the prayers we pray! He basically prays, God will bless Ruth in every way possible. He prays a very big prayer. And how does God answer that prayer? Through Boaz!

He uses the analogy that God is like a great bird protecting his daughter. Ruth had come to trust God and to rest under the refuge of God as a baby bird would rest under the wings of her parent.

A Confirmation of Faith

Ruth sees God's hand in all that she is experiencing. She's not getting ahead of herself. She's really giving thanks to Boaz for all his kindness.

> **Ruth 2:13** | Then she said, "I have found favor in your eyes, my lord, for you have comforted me and spoken kindly to your servant, though I am not one of your servants."

Ruth is unassuming. She doesn't say, "My ring is a size 6!" "What size is your tux?" She views herself as a servant of Boaz. She's content to be his servant.

Conclusion

Who does God use in our story? An old forgotten widow woman and a Gentile Moabite woman. God uses ordinary people. Sometimes we are quite less than ordinary, but that is just who God calls. Think about what Paul says in 1 Corinthians 1 that God only uses weak and foolish people. Even if he calls some of the mighty and wise, he has to crush them before he uses them.

> *1 Corinthians 1:26-31* | For consider your calling, brothers: not many of you were wise according to worldly standards, not many were powerful, not many were of noble birth. [27] But God chose what is foolish in the world to shame the wise; God chose what is weak in the world to shame the strong; [28] God chose what is low and despised in the world, even things that are not, to bring to nothing things that are, [29] so that no human being might boast in the presence of God. [30] And because of him you are in Christ Jesus, who became to us wisdom from God, righteousness and sanctification and redemption, [31] so that, as it is written, "Let the one who boasts, boast in the Lord."

God calls the weak, ordinary people so that we might boast only in the Lord! Let's boast in him! Amen.

3 | RUTH 2:14-23
TRUSTING GOD WITH OUR BLESSINGS

Naomi said to her daughter-in-law, "May he be blessed by the Lord, whose kindness has not forsaken the living or the dead!"
RUTH 2:20

When God blesses us, we have to remember that all of God's blessings are just an illustration of who God is. God is gracious and generous. But don't ever be deceived into being satisfied with blessings. Nothing, and I mean nothing will ever fully satisfy outside of Jesus Christ.

In Ruth 2 we have a picture of this. Boaz comes into the life of Ruth and begins to reflect the kindness and generosity of God! Isn't God good and gracious and kind? Here you have this starving Gentile woman, a very young widow, she's a foreigner in Israel, and someone welcomes her into the family of Israel. That someone's name is Boaz.

Charles Spurgeon said, "Jesus is our mighty Boaz." That's so true. He brings us into the family of God. He welcomes us into the throne room of his Father. And in him we have all spiritual blessings in heavenly places! We can say, "Blessed be the God and Father of our Lord Jesus Christ, who has blessed us in Christ with every spiritual blessing in the heavenly places" (Eph 1:3).

Don't get taken away with living for earthly blessings. Getting a degree in school is fine. Having a family is fine. Getting a job and making a living is fine. But we were not made for these things. We were made to live for the giver of those blessings.

Sometimes being blessed on this earth is the worst thing that can happen to us. The Puritan John Trapp said, "A ship may be overladen with silver, even unto sinking, and yet space enough be left to hold ten times more. So a covetous man, though he has enough to sink him, yet he never has enough to satisfy him."[19] Only Christ can satisfy. We need him in every part and every aspect of our being. St. Patrick the great evangelical missionary to Ireland had this motto: "Christ beside me, Christ before me, Christ behind me, Christ within me, Christ beneath me, Christ above me."[20] May Christ be our blessings and all other blessings be a reflection that he alone is lovely, and he alone satisfies.

The most dangerous place for a Christian is not in the valley when stripped of every blessing but Christ. Though they are the worst of times as human beings, they are often the best of times for Christian growth. The most dangerous place for a Christian is on the mountaintop when we are surrounded by blessings. It is then we tend to forget Christ and covet for more.

In our text, we come to Ruth 2, beginning with verse 14, and we find that Ruth and Naomi are about to receive some fantastic and amazing blessings from the Lord and they get to see that all our blessings are a result of God's kindness. We were God's enemies. Ruth is a Moabite. There are covenant curses against the Moabites. As believers we were all under the curse, but through the covenant kindness of Jesus, that curse has been lifted.

Ruth, now a believer, now in the covenant community of Israel gets to experience that kindness and blessing. But what do we do with God's blessings? We can't make them idols. This passage teaches us three things we can do with blessings: share your blessing (2:14-18), praise God for your blessings (2:19-22), and wait for God's blessing in God's time (2:23).

We come to Ruth 2:14, and Boaz is prominent in this verse. Remember Boaz is half Canaanite. His mother is Rahab, the former harlot from Jericho who became a believer and had her life transformed. Boaz

---

[19] I.D.E. Thomas, ed., *A Puritan Golden Treasury* (Carlisle, PA: Banner of Truth, 2000), 67.

[20] St. Patrck in Marilyn McEntyre, *Christ, My Companion Meditations on the Prayer of St. Patrick* (Eugene, OR: Wipf and Stock Publishers, 2012), 10.

is a man of wealth, wisdom, and war. He's a provider and protector. He's generous. He's reflecting the kindness of Yahweh. He's being conformed to his image.

SHARE YOUR BLESSINGS (2:14-16)

The Blessing of Servanthood

Even though Boaz is the boss, he acts like a servant to Ruth.

> **Ruth 2:14** | And at mealtime Boaz said to her, "Come here and eat some bread and dip your morsel in the wine." So she sat beside the reapers, and he passed to her roasted grain. And she ate until she was satisfied, and she had some left over.

Boaz is a single man. He owns this field. He's a good employer. He provides food for his employees. You can imagine perhaps other workers could smell the good grain being roasted in that field, wishing they could work for Boaz. He was a good man. He trusted God. He was good to his employees.

What does Boaz say to Ruth? "Come here and dip your morsel in the wine." She sat beside the reapers, a seat of respect and prominence and holiness, and he's really honoring her. And he passed her the roasted grain. Who served Ruth? Boaz. What is he? The boss. What is he doing serving her? You see the family resemblance here, with Jesus?

Though he's in charge, he's humble; he takes the posture of a servant. In that culture, the Moabite woman would have served the Hebrew men. Boaz says, "No, no, no. She's met the Lord. She's my sister in faith. She's a wonderful gal. Have a seat. I'm a gentleman; you're a lady. Let me serve you." Take note of that, men. Be a gentleman. Be a godly, generous, kind, humble, servant to all women. And, when God should bring along your wife, you will have treated her the way you should have because you treat all ladies the same way.

The equivalent would be the owner of a restaurant finding out that a homeless woman was a believer, and he brings her into the restaurant, sits her at the best table, and serves her. Isn't that what Jesus did?

> *2 Corinthians 8:9* | You know the grace of our Lord Jesus Christ, that though he was rich, yet for your sake he became poor, so that you by his poverty might become rich.

Boaz says essentially, "Order whatever you want." "Come here and eat some bread and dip your morsel in the wine." Boaz was generous with the blessings he received from God.

Isn't that how our glorious Boaz is? Whenever we go to Christ for our meal, like Ruth, we are completely satisfied. When Jesus is the host—no guest goes empty from the table. How full we are! Jesus fills our heart until it is at perfect peace; our mind with persuasion of the truth of his teachings; our memory with recollections of what he has done, and our imagination with the prospects of what he is yet to do.

We've been in dry seasons before, but like Ruth "was satisfied and had some left over" so is it with us. Now that we have sat at the table of the Lord's love, we can say, "Nothing but the infinite love of Jesus can ever satisfy me! I am such a great sinner—that I must have infinite merit to wash my sin away!" Let us magnify the generosity of our glorious Boaz![21]

The Blessing of Generosity

Ruth eats to her full, but of course, she thinks of her mother-in-law Naomi. She can't leave without something for her. Boaz makes sure of it. In her greatest time of need, where she is the only bread winner, God provides through the generosity of his saints. Praise God that God's people will always be provided for "according to his riches in glory by Christ Jesus" (Phil 4:19).

A Generous Meal

Ruth 2:14b | So she sat beside the reapers, and he passed to her roasted grain. And she ate until she was satisfied, and she had some left over.

Ruth was full. Best meal she's had in a long time. She's really blessed at this point. But she has food left over! Now, who, who is supposed to get that food? Naomi. Take note of this, gentlemen. You must not only court the woman. You also must court her mother. Boaz knew Ruth's faithful reputation. She had a dear, kind of adopted, mother at home. So Ruth has this big meal, and Boaz sends dessert home for Naomi, in a matter of speaking.

---

[21] Charles Spurgeon. *Morning and Evening*, March 19—Ruth 2:14.

A Generous Job

Boaz gives Ruth a job. There she was in a foreign village, Bethlehem, and by faith she trusts God. Like manna from heaven, she gets a job from Boaz.

Ruth 2:15 | "When she rose to glean, Boaz instructed his young men, saying, "Let her glean even among the sheaves, and do not reproach her."

She was to harvest as much of the corners of the field as she liked. This was a provision of the Mosaic law. The poor could gather as much from the corners of the fields as they wanted. Boaz made sure of it. But he went above and beyond for Ruth.

A Generous Bonus

Ruth 2:16 | "And also pull out some from the bundles for her and leave it for her to glean, and do not rebuke her."

Boaz is generous, not just by giving her a job, but he gives her a bonus, a pay raise. He tells the men to purposely leave already harvested sheaves – wheat stalks – for Ruth. She's going to bring a lot home to Naomi.

Boaz told his young men what to do. He's giving her plenty for herself and her dear mother-in-law, Naomi. I love that about Boaz! He tells young men what to do. Why? Young men do not know what to do. Right? Forty percent of young men don't even have a dad. Many of you who do have a dad, he doesn't tell you anything, or most of what he tells you is totally wrong. We need godly men who will lead. Boaz is that leader.

Look at Boaz. He loves to *share* his blessing. He's generous. She was dirt poor, and he feeds her probably the best meal of her life, gives her a job, and then gives her gleanings that would feed her and her house for a good while.

Many people view Christians as stingy, self-centered, and uncompassionate. David Kinnaman of the Barna Group presents statistical research and extensive interviews from a three-year study that document how an overwhelming percentage of sixteen to twenty-nine-year-olds view Christians with hostility, resentment, and disdain. It would be hard to overestimate, says Kinnaman, "how firmly people reject — and feel rejected by — Christians."[22] Christians should be known as the most caring and generous of all people.

The Blessing of Sharing

Not only is Boaz generous with Ruth, but Ruth is generous with her precious mother-in-law, Naomi. What does Ruth do, so that she can have an abundance to share? She works hard. You will see that Ruth is a woman who takes the opportunities that God gives her. She works hard. She acts holy. God continues to provide opportunities.

> **Ruth 2:17-18** | So she gleaned in the field until evening. Then she beat out what she had gleaned, and it was about an ephah of barley. **18** And she took it up and went into the city. Her mother-in-law saw what she had gleaned. She also brought out and gave her what food she had left over after being satisfied.

Now there's a debate as to what an ephah is. It is somewhere between maybe 30 and 50 pounds that she has obtained through her one day's labor. It was the equivalent, perhaps, of two weeks wages for the average worker. Here's what has happened. She just made a few thousand bucks in one day, without breaking the law!

How many young people tell their folks, "I'm going out to see if I can find a job today," and come home with a few thousand bucks?

PRAISE GOD FOR YOUR BLESSINGS (2:19-22)

One of the things that get us stuck in life and stunted in our Christian growth is a self-focused attitude. Wherever there is anger and fear, despair and a focus on worldly comfort, we know we've given Satan an "opportunity" (Eph 4:26-27). Joy and praise are the key evidence of the Spirit-filled life. Naomi, which means pleasantness or sweetness, lives up to her name.

Praise God for Provision

> **Ruth 2:19-20a** | And her mother-in-law said to her, "Where did you glean today? And where have you worked? Blessed be the man who took notice of you." So she told her mother-in-law with whom she had worked and said, "The man's name with whom I

---

[22] David Kinnaman. *UnChristian; What a New Generation Really Thinks About Christianity* (Grand Rapids: Baker Books, 2007), 19.

worked today is Boaz." **²⁰** And Naomi said to her daughter-in-law, "May he be blessed by the Lᴏʀᴅ, whose kindness has not forsaken the living or the dead!"

The woman who was bitter and broken becomes sweet again. This is Mara, the bitter woman who is now Naomi again, the worshipper of God. She is walking in the awareness of God's blessing again. Romans says that it's the kindness of God that leads to repentance (Rom 2:4). God has lovingly, graciously, kindly, mercifully, provided for Ruth and Naomi, and now Naomi's heart opens up.

The Provision of Divine Kindness

The one who said, "Don't call me sweetheart, call me bitter or wounded" is now praising God! Why? Because of God's *kindness*. That's an important word! In the Hebrew, it is *hesed*, which means "loyal" or "steadfast love" or "unconditional, unrelenting, never dying love."[23] It really is the big theme in this book. It means God's "covenant mercy," which "designates God's loyalty in fulfilling his promises and his covenant."[24] How can we not bless God when he loyally follows us with his love, ultimately displayed in the substitution of Christ for our sins. Bless God, saints! Spurgeon said, "When we bless God for mercies, we usually prolong them. When we bless God for miseries, we usually end them. Praise is the honey of life which a devout heart extracts from every bloom of providence and grace."[25]

Can I ask you, as you look at God's provision for you, are you a sweetheart or a bitter person? All you have to do to become sweet is look upon the cross of Jesus who gave everything for you. If you can't see that, then you cannot have the capacity for sweetness.

The Provision of Human Kindness

Ruth 2:20b | Naomi also said to her, "The man is a close relative of ours, one of our redeemers."

---

[23] *Hesed* is often translated "lovingkindness" or "tender mercies" in the KJV, but it is better rendered "steadfast love" as in the RSV and ESV.

[24] George Eldon Ladd, D. A. Hagner, ed., *A Theology of the New Testament*, Revised Edition (Grand Rapids, MI: William B. Eerdmans Publishing Company, 1993), 301.

[25] Charles Spurgeon in Doris & Bryan Curtis, *Inspirational Thoughts to Warm the Soul: Quotations, Stories, and More* (iUniverse: Bloomington, IN, 2011), 87.

Let me explain to you what a redeemer does. In Leviticus 25, a redeemer has two primary functions: to redeem people and property. In that culture, if you got yourself into debt, you couldn't just wrack up credit card debt or declare bankruptcy. You would either sell yourself or your land to pay off your debt. You would sell yourself into slavery for a period of time to work at no income to another person to pay off your debt, but that would devastate your family 'cause you would have no income. Or you would sell your land. Now, in selling your land, this is an agrarian society. People live on the farm. They work on the farm. They eat off the farm. The farm stays in the family for multiple generations.

So if the main bread winner died, in order not to lose the family and the land, God said a close relative must take the responsibility to raise up a seed and pay the debts and protect and provide.

Single men, if you are waiting for the perfect woman who has the perfect background and fits with you perfectly you'll be waiting a long time. And if you find her, let me tell you, she won't be interested in you!

You ought to be looking for a Ruth. She's been through some trials – and she's trusted the Lord. She's the Proverbs 31 woman. She's industrious. She is godly, has integrity. Boaz sees this and begins to provide for her and protect her. I don't know his motives. I believe he had no intentions underlying his motive except to be a godly man.

Men are supposed to provide and protect. Boaz is doing both. This is what makes a man to function as a man. Men, can I ask you, are you acting like a man? Who do men do? What makes a man masculine? Some of what you think of masculine is simply a very sad state of immature childishness. Some of it is pure evil and selfishness. What is it that makes a man function as a man? This is the definition of biblical masculinity by Wayne Grudem. Some of you have his volume on systematic theology. Here's what he says:

> At the heart of biblical masculinity is a sense of benevolent responsibility to lead, provide, and protect women in ways appropriate to a man's differing relationships.[26]

---

[26] Wayne Grudem, *Recovering Biblical Manhood & Womanhood: A Response to Evangelical Feminism* (Wheaton, IL: Good News Publishers, 2006), Kindle Locations 730-732.

Mature masculinity expresses itself not in the demand to be served, but in the strength to serve and to sacrifice for the good of woman. Jesus said, "Let the greatest among you become as the youngest and the leader as one who serves" (Lk 22:26). Humble leadership will have the holy aroma of heaven about it — the demeanor of Christ. This was Boaz' attitude. He was serving God first and foremost. He was not serving himself. That's something for Ruth and Naomi to praise God for! Boaz is put in this very strategic position of being the kinsman redeemer. His acts of kindness mirror those of God. He is God's instrument of blessing to Ruth and we will find out to the entire human race.

Praise God for Protection

Ruth says to Naomi, "The man's name with whom I worked today is Boaz" (2:19). Boaz means "strong man," "mighty man," "godly man," "masculine, defender, protector, provider." The cry of her heart, in Ruth 2:2, was that God would give her "favor" in the eyes of someone, and God has given her favor, grace, mercy in the eyes of Boaz. Boaz lives up to his name, and Ruth accounts that Boaz assigned a group of bodyguards for her.

> **Ruth 2:21** | And Ruth the Moabite said, "Besides, he said to me, 'You shall keep close by my young men until they have finished all my harvest.'"

Not only that, but Boaz himself is looking out for her. Remember we are in the time of the book of Judges. Most men are selfish abusers. Naomi knows Ruth is safe in Boaz' field. She says, "In another field you might be assaulted."

> **Ruth 2:22** | And Naomi said to Ruth, her daughter-in-law, "It is good, my daughter, that you go out with his young women, lest in another field you be assaulted."

Many of the women of that time were seductresses. They used their beauty to get their way. Here are two godly single people who are waiting on God. They are a bit older. They are not without their struggles and temptations. Boaz didn't use his wealth to "hurry" God's plan. Ruth didn't use her beauty to "hurry" God's plan. It's hard to wait! But wait they did. What sustained Ruth and Boaz? Ruth trusted God's *hesed*. They knew God would be faithful to his word. "If you trust in me and take refuge in me, you will not be disappointed." They waited on God because he keeps his word. Single men and women, don't trust your heart! Trust an almighty God of loyal love who keeps his word!

Wherever you are on earth, there are dangerous men out there. God protects Ruth, but how does he protect her? He uses Boaz and his men. What we have is a theological lesson on biblical manhood. God has given men by nature, great strength and positions of authority. We have a choice as to what to do with this authority. Spirit-filled men use their strength to protect and provide for the vulnerable.

WAIT FOR GOD'S BLESSING IN GOD'S TIME (2:23)

We learn that the end of barley harvest is coming, and Ruth has some hope, but she doesn't rush it. She's willing to wait on God. She teaches us how to wait on God's timing and not push our own way.

Wait with Fellowship

Ruth 2:23a | So she kept close to the young women of Boaz.

Ruth hung out with the women. You know what that means? She wasn't married. Where did she live? With her mother-in-law, Naomi. She kept close to the women. Many of prayers of Ruth and Naomi have been answered. They have a house now. They have food. They're not starving. God's been faithful. But there's no husband. No baby.

Do you know what Ruth's name means? It's almost cruel to think about it at this point in the book. Her name means "companion" and she's all alone. She was meant to be married, and it's clear she wants to be married, but she's content to be the companion of God, to have the Lord as her husband. But she has her believing friends in Israel. As you wait on God, stay close to your forever family in your local church. Be active in service with brothers and sisters who love Jesus.

Wait with Faithfulness

Ruth 2:23b | ...gleaning until the end of the barley and wheat harvests. And she lived with her mother-in-law.

Ruth stayed making an income in a way that was honoring to God. She could have taken the "easy" route to security. Ruth could have become a Moabite seductress, but she's not. She's faithful. She follows Yahweh even it means she'll starve because she believes he's faithful.

As far as Ruth is concerned, God doesn't owe her a husband. She determines God is faithful, and she's going to trust him. So here is the woman called "Companion" with no companion. We know the end of the story, but Ruth didn't.

What happens at the end of barley harvest? Everyone goes home. This is just a temp job. Ruth doesn't know the end of the story. As far as she's concerned, this looks like the end of the line. It feels like the end! Boaz shows up on the scene, and he feeds her. He prays for her. He pays her well for her labor. But then the story goes silent. He's like many of you who are kind to a woman, but you may not know what that means. Single men, you must not lead the woman on.

Someone has said that men chasing women are like dogs chasing fire engines. Should they get one, they're not sure what to do with it. You kind of see that here.

Had she rushed the blessing, she would have gotten a curse. We'll find out later that there was another kinsman that was more closely related to her. She's got six weeks left to harvest. But she doesn't rush God. This is what I love. She doesn't leave the place that God blesses. I would just encourage all of you to understand this. Some people say, "God bless me! Please, bless me, God!" Stay in the place that God blesses. She doesn't say, "Well, it's been six weeks. I'm going back to Moab. It's been six weeks. No, she stays faithful.

The equivalent today would be this: She lives a holy life. She goes to work. She pays her bills. She reads her Bible. She gets baptized. She joins the church. She has Christian friends. She lives in the place that God could bless. God doesn't bless disobedience. Live in the place of blessing. That's the place of faithfulness and obedience. Don't rush God. Wait on the Lord.

> *Psalm 27:14* | Wait on the Lord; be of good courage, and he shall strengthen your heart; wait, I say, on the Lord!

Conclusion

This past week, the mother of a dear saint passed away, and it brought me back to the time when I was 15 years old, and my mother at 49 passed away. I had just been saved, but immediately I had no one and nothing but God. And that's a good place to be. When you are stripped of everything, that's when God does his best work. Those times remind us that God is all we need so when the blessings come, we will not make them idols, but simply praise God for the blessings that flow from him!

4 | RUTH 3:1-18
TRUSTING GOD WITH NEW ENDEAVORS

At midnight the man was startled and turned over, and behold, a woman lay at his feet! He said, "Who are you?" And she answered, "I am Ruth, your servant. Spread your wings over your servant, for you are a redeemer." And he said, "May you be blessed by the Lord, my daughter.
RUTH 3:8-10

We all know the story of Ruth. It's really the story of a faithful Jewish woman named Naomi from Bethlehem (house of bread) and her husband Elimelech. There's a terrible famine in the land of Israel, and the "house of bread" becomes a "house of famine." She follows her husband Elimelech obediently to the pagan land of Moab. They don't want to die. Moab is only fifty miles away and is an oasis where they can get work and food, and everything seems to fall in place to live there. But when they get there, the paganism is out of control. The boys marry pagan, Moabite wives. And God's hand of blessing is removed from them. Elimelech, who moves to Moab in order to outmaneuver death, dies, and their two sons Mahon and Chilion (sick and dying) die as well! A very tragic story.

Of course, you know the story of Ruth is one of hope and redemption. After ten years in Moab, Naomi decides it's time to go back to Israel, back to Bethlehem, the house of bread. The famine has lifted.

There is a moment of decision. Ruth and Orpah want to be with Naomi. Naomi challenges them, tests their faith – says "Go back to Moab and serve your gods." Orpah leaves but remember the words of Ruth. This is Ruth's conversion. This is her confession that YHWH is Lord and Savior of her life.

> *Ruth 1:16-17* | Where you go I will go, and where you lodge I will lodge. Your people shall be my people, and your God my God. [17] Where you die I will die, and there will I be buried. May the Lord do so to me and more also if anything but death parts me from you."

This was a pledge of allegiance to Yahweh and his people. So Ruth is converted. This would be the equivalent of a young woman meeting the Lord and saying, "I want to go to your because I want to be a member of your church, where God's people love and serve the Lord. I need to get baptized; I want to get discipleship in a Bible Study. I want to have Christian friends. I desire to grow in my relationship with God." Ruth is gloriously converted!

And you also remember that Ruth and Naomi were on the brink of starvation and homelessness; and last week we saw how they went from starving and almost homeless, to blessed and highly favored. Naomi had said "Call me Mara" or *bitter, broken woman*. Ruth was sent out gleaning, and on the scene comes Boaz! And so she just *happens* to come upon a man Boaz, who loves the Lord. Boaz happens to be loaded with money. Boaz happens to be single. And Ruth just happens to choose the field of Boaz.

God promises to take care of this vulnerable, single, foreign Moabite young widow woman. She's as vulnerable as they come. God takes care of her. And God will take care of you. Oswald Chambers said this:

> In the midst of the [devastating trials], a touch comes, and you know it is the right hand of Jesus Christ. You know it is not the hand of restraint, correction, nor chastisement, but the right hand of the Everlasting Father. Whenever hle
>
> is hand is laid upon you, it gives inexpressible peace and comfort, and the sense that underneath are the everlasting arms (Deut 33:27), full of support, provision, comfort, and strength.[27]

---

[27] Oswald Chambers, *My Utmost for His Highest* (Barbour: Uhrichsville, OH, 2006), 24.

Boaz provided protection and provision for her and Naomi. Ruth realizes he's a kinsman redeemer. He can buy them out of debt and potential slavery. Everything is looking rosy. Boaz serves her a meal. Provides her with grain and food and protection.

And then.... Yes, that's right. Barley harvest is about to end, and nothing happens. It's just about the end of barley harvest. Ruth 2:23 tells us: "So she kept close to the young women of Boaz, gleaning until the end of the barley and wheat harvests. And she lived with her mother-in-law." Ruth goes to her job, but it's only a

job. Barley harvest is about over. She works for Boaz every day for six or seven weeks. Boaz shows kindness to her. He prays for her. He protects her. He's a gentleman. He's a godly, worthy man. But he doesn't follow up. He doesn't call. Ruth is kind of left hanging. There was a time where he elevated her – he gave her as a foreigner the highest seat with the best food. In my mind sparks were flying. This could be the one! I was already ringing the wedding bells.

But they never have a "second meeting." Boaz doesn't call. Barley harvest is about over. Nothing. Boaz is like the average guy. He does not know how to close the deal. He does not follow through. Ruth must be thinking: "Where are we? Are we friends? Are we more than friends? What are we?" They need to define the relationship. But Ruth is left hanging.

I don't think Boaz was purposely negligent of Ruth. He was a gentleman. Ruth is a Moabite. This is complicated. I'm sure Boaz is thinking, *"Another lonely barley harvest! All this grain and no one to share it with!"* What should he do? Barley harvest is ending. Boaz is a gentleman, likely being cautious. What can Ruth do? She's a Moabite! What rights does she have in Israel right now? If anything is done, Naomi must do it. God is about to call Ruth and Boaz to a new endeavor. And we are going to find out about four things God calls us to in a new endeavor.

OBEDIENCE IN NEW ENDEAVORS (3:1-5)

God calls Ruth to obey Naomi in a very radical thing: moving to a new country, following God by faith. God always requires obedience when he gives us a new endeavor. Let's see how this plays out in Ruth's life. During the weeks of the barley and wheat harvests (*cf* 2:23), Naomi had time to put her plan together. When the time was right, she acted.

Obedience Requires Humility

Ruth 3:1-2 | Then Naomi her mother-in-law said to her, "My daughter, should I not seek rest for you, that it may be well with you? **2** Is not Boaz our relative, with whose young women you were? See, he is winnowing barley tonight at the threshing floor."

Naomi has a plan, but it means nothing if Ruth doesn't trust her. The plan is for Ruth to let Boaz know she is available for marriage. To "seek rest" is literally to seek a home, (*cf* 1:9). In other words, Ruth was to seek to be settled and secure in a home with a husband.[28] For Naomi's plan to succeed, Ruth had to trust her entirely, listening and receiving what Naomi says with a spirit of humility. Ruth later gladly expresses this humble faith (3:5, "All that you say I will do").

Naomi's plan reveals that she is now resolved to have her daughter-in-law make herself available for marriage to Boaz. Ruth had formerly given up the possibility of remarriage in order to care for the aging Naomi, but now marriage suddenly again became a possibility. It was customary for Hebrew parents to arrange marriages for their children (Jdg 14:1–10).

Ruth wants to take care of Naomi, and now knowing Boaz is a possibility, from Naomi's perspective the chief way to do that is to give Naomi an heir. The problem is: *Ruth's not married!* She's got two options at this point. One is the way of Scripture, and if she had a godly father, this is where the godly father would get involved. And he would go meet with Boaz, "Boaz, you love the Lord. My daughter really likes you. It seems like you like her. Where are we going? What are we doing? I need to see your doctrinal statement, your 401k. Do you love Jesus? Do you have a job? We need to see if you're the one." And the father was to get involved.

The way it works in Scripture, it says that men seek or take a wife, and that daughters are given in marriage. That's the language of the Bible. Genesis says that a man will leave his father and mother; he is then to get a job, get a house, get a clue, get a theology, get a church, get himself together, and then he is to pursue a woman for marriage, and that her family is to be involved, making sure that she is married to a good and godly man. The father is to guide the process, to give his

---

[28] Reed, "Ruth," in *The Bible Knowledge Commentary*, 424.

daughter in marriage. We show this by the father walking a daughter down the aisle. He's saying, "I've provided and protected you, and now I'm handing that responsibility off to another man."

The problem for Ruth is she doesn't have that kind of father, like many of you ladies. We know nothing of her dad. We've heard not a word of her dad. She left Moab – if she had a dad, he's not a believer. He's a Moabite. And their race and their religion are essentially intertwined, one and the same. She moves to Bethlehem, she comes without even a shekel in her pocket, or a bite to eat. If she has a father, he has not loved her, protected her, or provided for her. He's not supported her. He's not done anything. She is on her own. Can God still work in this situation? Yes!

Plan B for her could have been the Moabite way, also known as the Chicagoite way (or whatever city you live in)! The Moabites were a lascivious, promiscuous, confused people, kind of like people from the USA. We are three thousand years removed from the story of Ruth, but the way that her people that she comes from conduct themselves in dating and marital situations is much like our own.

By the way, *dating* was a word that was introduced into the American language in 1896 as lower-class slang for prostitution. So, to say, "I'm going out on a date" means I'm picking up my prostitute.

In the early 1900s, women would enter into a relationship of courtship and engagement and marriage through what was known as calling, whereby the man would come to the woman's house and spend time with the woman and her mother and her father, and his gun, and they would all get together and they would sip tea and visit, and the boy could only come if he had an appointment, and as soon as the appointment was over he would have to leave. And he was in the woman's safe home environment with her family.

A woman was very concerned about her reputation, so much so that she wouldn't go out into public, even with a brother or an uncle or a cousin, alone if she was single, because she wouldn't want to give the impression that she was out on a date, acting like a prostitute.

What happened then was that women's magazines started to come out beginning with things like the Ladies Home Journal, which quickly sold a million copies, and now you've got voices competing with the mother and the father, telling the woman, "Here's how you should dress, and here's what men to like, and here's how you can get one," and it was just like the junk that's lining the grocery store check-out line shelves, as we speak. In the 1920s you had automobiles and urbanization. A car is a closet on wheels. In the 1930s restaurants sprouted up. Kids traveled farther from the home and the influence of parents. In the 1940s feminism begins with World War II. Women wanted to become more like men. In the 1950s, you had the birth of "rock and roll" and promiscuity was openly promoted in music. The 1960s brought us the sexual revolution, the birth control pill, "free love", and a lot of moral confusion. In the 1970s magazines of ill-repute would now be sold openly at the gas stations. In 1973 abortion is legalized. In 1974 comes the no fault divorce. In 2015 same sex marriage was legalized.

The result is that our nation has a very Moabite culture. You and I are born into a world that we think is normal because it's all we know. But it is not *normal*. It's not Christlike. It's very Moabite. So Ruth takes the counsel of an older woman, Naomi. This is sort of echoing the concept of Titus 2: older woman gives counsel to younger.

God's plan is different. Ruth doesn't have a father on the scene. She's not going back to her old life and her old ways. What can she do? Nothing! She's a Moabite. Naomi gets involved. Naomi wants to "seek rest" for Ruth. She wants to set her up in marriage! Let's hear the details of the plan. We'll find that Naomi gives Ruth so strange instructions.

Ruth is powerless to help herself. Naomi must do something. And something she does! Naomi lifts Ruth to a new endeavor and gives her some specific instructions.

Obedience Requires Action

> **Ruth 3:3a** | Wash therefore and anoint yourself, and put on your cloak and go down to the threshing floor.

Ruth is given four commands by Naomi. She was to "wash." Ruth needed to clean herself up because up to this time Ruth's been working in the field. All Boaz has seen is her sweaty, smelly, no makeup, messed up hair. You get the idea. She was also to "anoint" herself with perfume. Romance is in the air! Then Ruth was told, "Put on your cloak." Get some nice clothes on. Forget the factory uniform, so to speak. This is a major shift in Ruth's life. Up to this time she and Naomi have been in mourning. It's time for both of them to put off the clothes of mourning and put on the clothes of a new day! You may be living in regret for the past. What can you do about the past? You can certainly ask God for forgiveness, but you surely cannot change the past. There comes a point when it's time to move on. For Ruth, her clothing signaled that it was a new day. The "cloak" also would be a larger outer garment so that Ruth would have been less recognizable, in case this plan of Naomi's doesn't work out. With a larger outer garment, Ruth would be able to slip away unnoticed. And the fourth things she was told was to "go down to the threshing floor." This was a great act of obedient faith for Ruth.

The point is, Ruth is willing to follow Naomi as Naomi follows Yahweh. What incredible faith for Ruth. Barley harvest is ending. Boaz is kind of paralyzed. This is a Moabite woman. I'm not sure he knows what to do. Ruth can't do much. She's a Moabite. This is the place where most of us panic, right? We take things into our own hands. Not Ruth. In the midst of great possibilities and seeming blindness on Boaz's part, she waits on God and walks with God. She listens to the voice of her mother-in-law. Ruth learns to obey Naomi, and really, she is living out her obedience to Naomi's God.

God calls Ruth to put away the mourning clothes and by faith, move on to a new stage and a new endeavor in her life. She is likely scared. But she trusts God and she trusts Naomi. She does all that Naomi says. Was it scary for Ruth? You bet! Courage is not the absence of fear but the ability to say no to fear and not allow it to control us. Her creed was later articulated by her great, great grandson, King David, "What time I am afraid, I will put my trust in you" (Pas 56:3).

Obedience Requires Courage

Ruth was to go down to where Boaz was. What Naomi asks of her is going to require great courage. We're going to see that the courage needed to obey God comes not by looking at circumstances or even to our leaders, but to God himself. Ruth's eyes were on Yahweh. Listen to Naomi's instructions to Ruth.

> **Ruth 3:3b** | "Go down to the threshing floor, but do not make yourself known to the man until he has finished eating and drinking.

Ruth was to go to the threshing floor in her large cloak, and she was not to make herself known to anyone. After Boaz finished eating and drinking, Ruth was to observe the place where he retired for the night.

Under cover of darkness Ruth was to go to Boaz, uncover his feet, and lie down there.

> **Ruth 3:4** | But when he lies down, observe the place where he lies. Then go and uncover his feet and lie down, and he will tell you what to do."

Naomi tells Ruth to go to the place where Boaz, after a good harvest meal, and "uncover his feet". What does that mean? Some have accused Ruth of returning to her Moabite ways in seduction, but nothing could be further from the truth. Ruth was recognized by everyone as "worthy woman" of noble character (3:11). The uncovering of the feet was a ceremonial act that was completely proper. It was an act that communicated that she was available for marriage. The scene took place in the dark so that Boaz had the opportunity to reject Ruth's availability without the whole town knowing about it.[29] Boaz would let her know if he was on board with Naomi's plan. This would be up to him. What a plan that Naomi presented to Ruth! How would Ruth respond?

Obedience Requires Faith

> **Ruth 3:5** | And she replied, "All that you say I will do."

In this statement: "All that you say I will do" (3:5), there is worship and trust of almighty God. I like Nancy Leigh DeMoss description of worship.

> Worship is a believer's response to God's revelation of himself. It is expressing wonder, awe, and gratitude for the worthiness, the greatness, and the goodness of our Lord. It is the appropriate response to God's person, his provision, his power, his promises, and his plan.[30]

We see that Ruth was looking beyond Naomi, and looking to Naomi's God, the one true God. With that kind of transcendent faith, she could gladly say to Naomi, "All that you say I will do" (3:5). Jesus said, "If you love me, keep my commandments" (Jn 14:15). Ruth desires to obey God in total surrender. She therefore parts with her security and becomes even more vulnerable. Naomi knows the laws of the kinsman redeemer. I don't believe any woman in her right mind would want to

---

[29] Reed, "Ruth," in *The Bible Knowledge Commentary*, 425.
[30] Nancy Leigh DeMoss, *A Place of Quiet Rest: Finding Intimacy with God Through a Daily Devotional Life* (Chicago: Moody Press, 2009), 211.

do something so risky. But Ruth is now converted. She wants to obey God. She trusts Naomi. She puts off the mourning clothes. She puts on her clothes for a new day and a new life. And she trusts God, following a weak but faithful woman named Naomi, knowing that almighty God is in absolute control. Ruth may lose everything, but she wants to obey God. She trusts God because she knows God wants her highest happiness. Thomas Watson said, "God would have us part with nothing for him, but that which will damn us if we keep it. He has no design upon us, but to make us happy."[31]

Note this as well. We find out Ruth's motives here are not marriage. We know that by the very language she uses in the passage. In verse 10, Boaz later calls what she is doing an act of "kindness" (חסד). He says, "You have made this last kindness greater than the first." The first act of "kindness" is best understood to be Ruth's loyalty to her mother-in-law that led her to leave her own country (2:10).[32] Her second act of kindness was to Boaz, being willing to follow God in faith into marriage. Obedience must be our motive. We might say that Ruth was willing to "seek first the kingdom of heaven" and all that God wanted for her was added to her (Mt 6:33). Indeed God withholds nothing good from his children who are following in obedient faith.

> *Psalm 84:11* | The LORD God is a sun and shield; the LORD bestows favor and honor. No good thing does he withhold from those who walk uprightly.

SURPRISES IN NEW ENDEAVORS (3:6-9)

What we have in verses 6-9 is a lot of surprises, mainly for Boaz. He gets the surprise of his life when he finds a woman at his feet. I love God's promise to Jeremiah.

> *Jeremiah 33:3* | Call to me and I will answer you, and will tell you great and hidden things that you have not known.

In other words, God loves surprises. And this story brings some very surprising instructions from Naomi.

---

[31] A Puritan Golden Treasury, compiled by I.D.E. Thomas, Banner of Truth, Carlisle, PA. 2000, p. 159.

[32] Robert L. Hubbard, Jr.., *The Book of Ruth*, "NICOT" (Grand Rapids: Eerdmans, 1988), 463.

Surprising Instructions

Ruth 3:6 | So she went down to the threshing floor and did just as her mother-in-law had commanded her.

Naomi has given some very scary counsel to Ruth. Now let's understand that Naomi's counsel is descriptive not prescriptive. That is, what she says is not what you should do, but it is what she told Ruth to do in this very special situation. So, Ruth obeys, and she has no idea what's going to happen. She's doing this not for herself but for her mother-in-law. Ruth has no idea how all of this is going to turn out, but she doesn't need to worry. She's trusting God, and she knows God loves surprises. So far, Ruth has experienced so many surprises. She's received a job and a bonus and a home to live in. God's been so good. Why shouldn't she expect him to do even greater things?

In Israel, this is the time of great celebration. It is the festival of harvest time. In the Old Testament it was called the Feast of Weeks, or the Feast of the Harvest. This is the Thanksgiving time in Israel. There's tons of food. Tons of people. Lots of celebration. And at the end of the day, Boaz is going to sleep by the grain. And what a surprise he has coming!

Ruth goes down to the threshing floor as Naomi had instructed her. It's a hard packed floor. The harvesters have brought in all the grain. They trample it with animals or with sledgehammers or with carts. They would break the husk. They would then get a fork, a pitchfork, or a shovel. They would throw the grain into the air. The wind would blow the chaff away. The heavier grain would fall to the ground. This was the center of the party. This is where everyone is celebrating. Everybody is thanking God. And as the sun is setting, the happy day is concluding, and Boaz has a nice big meal. That's when Ruth takes her step of faith, and she has no idea what surprises await her.

A Surprising Reunion

Ruth 3:6-8 | So she went down to the threshing floor and did just as her mother-in-law had commanded her. ⁷ And when Boaz had eaten and drunk, and his heart was merry, he went to lie down at the end of the heap of grain. Then she came softly and uncovered his feet and lay down. ⁸ At midnight the man was startled and turned over, and behold, a woman lay at his feet!

"At midnight..." This doesn't even sound good! Whoa! There's a woman! Boaz is surprised!

Ruth 3:9a | He said, "Who are you?"

Good question! Historically, at harvest time, prostitutes would also come out to the threshing floor. It was payday. The prostitutes would take advantage of that. It's night. Boaz doesn't recognize Ruth. She smells good. She's got a large outer garment on to further disguise her. Boaz doesn't call her Ruth. He says, "Who are you?" "Who's that woman down there?" Smells like trouble.

Ruth 3:9b | And she answered, "I am Ruth, your servant."

Sweet Ruth. Here? That's a surprise. She presents herself to Boaz as, "Your servant." Before she had called herself "a foreigner" (2:10), but now she says she is a servant, or "a woman who is marriageable – a maidservant of Israel." for Boaz' consideration.[33] She now understands her identity in Yahweh.

It must also be noted that this is Ruth's description of herself: she is very intentional in convey herself as a woman who is desirable for marriage.[34] By the end of this scene Ruth will have moved all the way from a foreigner to a "woman of noble character" (3:11); this progression is obvious. It gets even more amazing.

A Surprising Proposal

We continue reading our story of Ruth, and we see an incredible trust in the Lord that gives her courage. She now brings up the Mosaic law. She is a godly woman, and she knows the Scriptures. Boaz is a kinsman redeemer.

Ruth 3:9c | "Spread your wings over your servant, for you are a redeemer."

In chapter 2, verse 12, Boaz had prayed that God would take her under his proverbial wing. And here she is saying, "Boaz, why don't you answer that prayer and be God's wing. Love me, protect me, hold me

---

[33] DeMoss, *A Place of Quiet Rest*, 211.
[34] K. Lawson Younger, Jr., *Judges and Ruth*, "NIVAC" (Grand Rapids: Zondervan, 2002), 461.

close, look after me." Here we have a metaphor. In ancient Jewish culture, to propose marriage a Jewish man would put a blanket over his potential bride. Does Ruth propose to Boaz? No. But she proposes that *he* propose!

This is an amazing sacrifice for Ruth. she is crossing here a number of taboos. A woman asking a man, a Moabite asking a Hebrew, a younger person asking an older person, an employee asking an employer. She's very bold. She takes a great risk. Her heart is not on marriage. This is very risky. It's almost insane. She's doing it for Naomi. She wants to take care of her mother-in-law. Motives are important. We must never be self-focused but God-focused. Being God-focused will give you immeasurable wisdom and boldness (Pro 9;10).

The question then begs to be answered, how will Boaz respond? How would you, gentlemen, respond? Some of you are single. Imagine being in the situation that Boaz is in. What do you say? Do you try and manipulate that towards sin? Will you act in sacrifice and holiness for the Lord?

WISDOM IN NEW ENDEAVORS (3:10-14)

Obviously, this situation calls for wisdom. You can see that Boaz doesn't have time to do a Bible study in this surprising situation. No, he has stored God's word in his heart and practiced the life of holiness his entire life. Wisdom is always granted to those who fear the Lord (Pro 1:7; 10:9).

The Wisdom of Prayer

Ruth 3:10a | And he said, "May you be blessed by the LORD, my daughter."

What's Boaz's response to this very unusual situation? "Anything I can pray for you about?" That shows his motives and his worthiness right there. He does not take advantage of her. He's openly bringing the Lord into the conversation. This is what we should do anytime we as noble men are in a questionable situation with a woman. As Boaz see this dear woman, he calls the Lord to join them in their conversation. What wisdom! And he expresses utter humility.

The Wisdom of Humility

Ruth 3:10b | You have made this last kindness greater than the first in that you have not gone after young men, whether poor or rich.

Boaz basically says, "I can't believe you'd want to be with me." I think Boaz is shocked that Ruth is interested in him. He's probably not the best-looking guy. But here's what he has: a job, literacy. He's a believer. He loves God. He's faithful. He's good to people, and he's going to be a faithful provider for his family. Boaz wasn't pursing Ruth perhaps because he did not feel he was worthy of her. That's humility.

Ladies, sometimes a man doesn't pursue you, not because he's not interested, but because he doesn't think that you would be interested in him. So Boaz is like, "You want to be with me? Done! I'm in!" What wisdom comes from that kind of humility.

The Wisdom of Holiness

Boaz now recognizes that this is a holy woman who loves the Lord.

Ruth 3:11 | And now, my daughter, do not fear. I will do for you all that you ask, for all my fellow townsmen know that you are a worthy woman.

In calling her a worthy woman he is echoing what was said of him in chapter 2, verse 1, that he was a worthy man, worthy of respect and praise and emulation. He's a good man, and now, he recognizes that she too is a woman of exceedingly good character.

In Proverbs 31 the same word is used of the prototypical Proverbs 31 woman. And here it's applied to the redeemed Moabite, Ruth. Remember after Proverbs 31 in the Hebrew Bible is the book of Ruth. One of my favorite verses really sums up the essence of a godly woman.

Proverbs 31:30 | Charm is deceitful, and beauty is vain, but a woman who fears the Lord is to be praised.

The most important attribute in a woman is not her past, but her present walk of holiness with the Lord. This woman, just a year before, was an unbeliever, and was a Moabite, and probably worshipping Chemosh. And now she loves the Lord. And she's had such a massive transformation that though she was a woman in sin and a woman who didn't know God, and a woman who didn't come from a good family, and a woman who didn't get a great start, she becomes a woman who is Proverbs 31, worthy of respect, worthy of praise, worthy of love, worthy of the commitment of Boaz. She's a woman of exceedingly good character. Jesus loves to do that for both men and women.

It's important to recognize that Boaz would have known of how God can radically transform an immoral woman, because his own mother is Rahab. She had been a prostitute in Jericho but had put her faith in Yahweh and become a notable woman of noble character in Israel. Tradition says that Rahab married one of the two spies, named Salmon. This is consistent with the Biblical record.[35]

Imagine the stories Boaz heard as he grew up. And imagine how having a mother who had been a foreigner and a harlot yet was grafted into the olive tree of Israel by the grace of God, affected the way Boaz viewed Ruth that day he saw her gleaning in his field. Other men might have simply seen a foreign woman scrounging for food, like a parasite. But Boaz saw something familiar and dear in a woman who had left her family, her nation, and her gods, to embrace Naomi, her nation, and her God. It seems Boaz was uniquely prepared by God for Ruth and Ruth for Boaz. Isn't that beautiful? A marriage made in heaven.

The Wisdom of Modesty

In the conversation Boaz has with Ruth, he demonstrates his modesty in a couple of ways. First, he doesn't think that he's necessarily going to be the one that would redeem Ruth.

> **Ruth 3:12-13** | And now it is true that I am a redeemer. Yet there is a redeemer nearer than I. **13** Remain tonight, and in the morning, if he will redeem you, good; let him do it. But if he is not willing to redeem you, then, as the Lord lives, I will redeem you. Lie down until the morning."

Boaz knows the town of Bethlehem well. It's just a little town, remember? His mom raised him there, and he knows the town and Naomi's deceased husband's family. There is a redeemer that is nearer in the bloodline than Boaz. He's not rushing ahead and making plans. He's not twisting the facts to try to get what he wants. He's patiently waiting on the Lord which displays a delightful modesty for a man.

---

[35] From the biblical record, it appears that Boaz's father was Salmon, and his mother was Rahab (Ruth 4:21, 1 Chron 2:11, Mt 1:5).

Second, Boaz doesn't call Ruth out. He doesn't take advantage of her. Consider how very wise he is in protecting Ruth's reputation.

> **Ruth 3:14** | So she lay at his feet until the morning, but arose before one could recognize another. And he said, "Let it not be known that the woman came to the threshing floor."

Boaz gave no hint that Ruth had embarrassed him by her actions or that she had done something that was not within her rights or against the customs of the day. Rather than thinking suggestive thoughts as some might have done in such a setting, he immediately blessed Ruth and protected her. As the sun rose, he urged her to depart. Boaz did not want her life complicated by village gossips, so he urged her not to let it be known she had been at the threshing floor. Nothing had happened that was improper, but gossipers are not careful about facts.[36]

FAITH IN NEW ENDEAVORS (3:15-18)

Imagine the joy and wonder in Ruth's heart as she departed the threshing floor early that morning before the sun rose. Heart racing, face flush. You know she's in love. And Boaz demonstrates his love. Again, we see him loading Ruth down with more grain. This was the currency of the time. Boaz is a picture of financial stability and generosity.

God's Past Faithfulness

As she is loaded down with so much grain, she must have been considering how God was faithful to take care of her thus far. God had been faithful!

> **Ruth 3:16** | And he said, "Bring the garment you are wearing and hold it out." So she held it, and he measured out six measures of barley and put it on her. Then she went into the city.

Boaz loaded her down with blessing. Take this and take this! Six measures of barley. Ruth had gone from a pagan idol worshipper filled with fear and anguish to a poor woman of faith, that was overflowing with blessing. God is so good. Look back on all God has brought you

---

[36] Reed, "Ruth," in *The Bible Knowledge Commentary*, 425.

through and brought you to, and rejoice in God's faithfulness to you in the past.

God's Present Faithfulness

Ruth goes back to her little home in little Bethlehem, and she tells the entire amazing story to her dear mother-in-law Naomi.

> **Ruth 3:16-17** | And when she came to her mother-in-law, she said, "How did you fare, my daughter?" Then she told her all that the man had done for her, [17] saying, "These six measures of barley he gave to me, for he said to me, 'You must not go back empty-handed to your mother-in-law.'"

Boaz is concerned about his possible mother-in-law. He not only blesses Ruth but blesses her family. What a vital trait for any suitor. You are not only courting the woman but her family as well. Beware of doing anything that you wouldn't want your affectionate mother to know. Look at all the Lord the Lord was doing to show his faithfulness to Ruth and Naomi, not only in the past, but also in the present.

God's Future Faithfulness

But there is still an unresolved matter looming overhead. What will happen with this other kinsman redeemer that is closer in the bloodline to Ruth? There are obviously sparks that are flying between Boaz and Ruth. They've put God first. They've honored one another. They've honored each other's families. Can they trust God with Ruth's future? Naomi gives good counsel to Ruth to "wait." Waiting on the Lord is the greatest demonstration of faith. Listen to Naomi.

> **Ruth 3:18** | She replied, "Wait, my daughter, until you learn how the matter turns out, for the man will not rest but will settle the matter today."

They are waiting on God and on godly men. Look at how God uses godly men in his providence. God's hand is seen in the heart and life of men like Boaz. Naomi tells Ruth, "Boaz will not rest till the matter is settled." The way this man settles issues is how all godly men ought to act. When we are ready to make the decision, we should make no delays. Defer nothing till tomorrow what can be done today. Do the hard thing first.

So we have just relived this exciting, surprising story, and we don't yet have a resolution. They're all waiting. Ruth, Naomi waiting at home. Boaz is waiting at the gate. This is what it is to follow God in a new endeavor. There's a lot of that kind of waiting in the Christian life.

It's like the pillar of fire in Israel. You don't move till you see the cloudy pillar of fire moving. That's God's *shekinah* (manifest) glory! Jesus said, "I am the light of the world" (Jn 8:12). If you know the history, he's talking at the Feast of Tabernacles. He's saying, "I'm the pillar of fire." Follow me! If God led Ruth thus far, he would lead her all the way. Regardless of how things would play out, Ruth and Naomi would be taken care of. If the closer redeemer wouldn't fulfill his duty, then Boaz had said, "If he is not willing to redeem you, then, as the Lord lives, I will re-deem you" (3:13). Boaz, like the Lord, promises to take care of us. I can't help but recall the words of Paul to the Philippians.

> *Philippians 1:6* | He who began a good work in you will carry it on to completion until the day of Christ Jesus.

Conclusion

We can trust our faithful God, just like Ruth and Boaz did. Boaz was a kinsman redeemer. In Old Testament Law, this meant that a near relative had the right to act on behalf of a person in trouble or in danger. When persons or possessions were in the grip of a hostile power, the kinsman might act to redeem (to win release and freedom). This could mean that the kinsman was required to marry the widow and purchase the widow's land.

A marriage of Boaz to Ruth would involve buying back Naomi's family land and meant that a possible son would carry on Naomi's family line.

Jesus, by taking on humanity, became our near Kinsman with the right to redeem you and me.[37] As Ruth offered herself in surrender to Boaz, so we offer ourselves in surrender to Christ, our true Boaz. As Ruth leaves herself at Boaz's mercy, so we are at Christ's mercy. As she was covered by Christ's garment, so we are covered in the righteousness of Christ. As she waits for Boaz to return, so we wait for Christ to return!

---

[37] Lawrence O. Richards, *The Teacher's Commentary* (Wheaton, IL: Victor Books, 1987), 193.

5 | RUTH 4:1-12
TRUSTING GOD WITH OBSTACLES

Boaz said, "The day you buy the field from the hand of Naomi, you also acquire Ruth the Moabite, the widow of the dead, in order to perpetuate the name of the dead in his inheritance." Then the redeemer said, "I cannot redeem it for myself, lest I impair my own inheritance. Take my right of redemption yourself, for I cannot redeem it.
RUTH 4:5-6

In this life, there are many setbacks on our way to glory. That's the whole point of the book of Ruth. Our lives as believers are not a straight line to glory, but we do eventually get there. Along the way there are many obstacles, but Jesus promises to overcome every one of them.

It reminds me of William Carey who was an English cobbler but would eventually translate the Bible for the people of India. Though he was a humble shoemaker, at the age of 32 he ventured off as a missionary to India. His motto was, "Expect great things from God—attempt great things for God." He learned several languages including Hebrew and Greek and translated the Bible into Bengali, Sanskrit, and numerous other Indian languages and dialects.

One of the greatest obstacles Carey faced was on 11 March 1812 when a fire in his print shop destroyed all of his translation of Sanskrit literature and a dictionary of Sanskrit and related languages. He had to have this before he translated the Bible. Yet it didn't stop him! In Carey's lifetime, the mission printed and distributed the Bible in whole or part in Sanskrit and 43 other languages and dialects.

The test of your character is what it takes to stop you. There are many disappointments in the Christian life. None of them are designed to cripple us. They are intended to make us more reliant on God and more conformed to the image of Jesus Christ.

I'll say it again. In this life, there are many setbacks on our way to glory. We see this in the story of Ruth and Naomi. Elimelech tried to avoid obstacles at all costs. He ran to Moab. We see something entirely different with Boaz and Ruth. Boaz goes into the teeth of the obstacles, and deals with setbacks in a godly, self-controlled, shrewd, honest, and biblical way.

The story in chapter 4 brings us into the jaws of a crisis. There was land in Naomi's family. They are in a bind. She's either needing to sell it right now so she can life, or perhaps more likely, Elimelech could have sold it before he moved his family to Moab. Either way, they are facing homelessness and being totally destitute. Leviticus 25 is clear that a near relative, a kinsman, needs to redeem the land for the widow and raise up a family, and Deuteronomy 25 says that he has to redeem the land and settle that family on the land.

What do we do when we come to an obstacle in the will of God? It often happens. In our study we will learn that when facing obstacles, we are to submit to authority (4:1-6), check our motives (4:7-10), and seek God in prayer (4:11-12).

Our story opens with Boaz at the gate of Bethlehem. This is where the town's elders would be seated. Boaz is a self-motivated person. He's just spent a night with Ruth, and he didn't touch her. She proposed that he propose to her, and what happens next? There are obstacles. Ruth is a bit forward (for the sake of Naomi). That's an obstacle. We find out there is a redeemer that is a closer relative than Boaz. That's an obstacle. Ruth has been married before, and she's now a widow. That's an obstacle. Ruth so far has been barren and has no children. That's an obstacle.

Boaz just spent the night with Ruth. They don't have any intimate relations, they don't move in together, there's nothing like that. He keeps his hands off her and waits to be married. The next day Boaz gets up and goes into town and sits by the gate.

SUBMIT TO AUTHORITY (4:1-6)

What a beautiful thing to see a marriable man submit to authority. One thing I've seen in marriages that fail, is they begin by skirting parental authority. Boaz is a man that is submitted to authority in his life. He trusts God, and therefore he trust the authority God has put over him.

The Priority of Authority

Ruth 4:1a | Now Boaz had gone up to the gate and sat down there.

We can see that Boaz is highly motivated, so he shows his trust in God by going directly to his God-given authority. He had every temptation to go around his authority. It's clear he's completely smitten by Ruth. Remember what he had told her?

Ruth 3:10 | May you be blessed by the Lord, my daughter. You have made this last kindness greater than the first in that you have not gone after young men, whether poor or rich.

Ruth could have had anyone, but Boaz is glad she is interested in him. Boaz had called the Lord's unrelenting love (*hesed*) to account (here translated "kindness") through Ruth. This lets us in on perhaps that Boaz thought he was out of Ruth's league. Boaz is so surprised Ruth would go for him. Here we see Boaz is older. He's probably not all that good looking. He's rich. He has a job. He loves Jesus. He's single. But he's humble. Such a man does exist! So he sits down at the gate. He wastes no time. He wants to marry Ruth. He feels unworthy to marry this Moabite woman. That's humility, and we know how God blesses humility (1 Pet 5:5).

Boaz doesn't try to skirt the Mosaic law. He doesn't take her unlawfully out of the hands of the man who is a closer kinsman to Ruth. He is a man of integrity who follows authority and follows the law. Romans 13:1 says, "The powers that be are ordained of God." God ordains authority. So Boaz calls a meeting with the elders of the city. He takes his case before his authorities.

5 | Ruth 4:1-12
Trusting God with Obstacles

Ruth 4:1 | Now Boaz had gone up to the gate and sat down there. And behold, the redeemer, of whom Boaz had spoken, came by. So Boaz said, "Turn aside, friend; sit down here." And he turned aside and sat down.

Boaz meets the unnamed redeemer. It is translated "friend" here, but in Hebrew it is literally, "Mr. So and So." Boaz wants to marry Ruth. But here's the complication. There's a huge obstacle. Boaz is not legally first in line with the right to marry Ruth. There's another guy who's got the right to marry her first. And so, between Boaz and Ruth and their happily ever after marriage, is a man who has legal right to marry Ruth before Boaz. He doesn't get a name because he's essentially Mr. Nobody. But he has the right to marry Ruth, and so Boaz has to deal with this obstacle.

Single men, when you love a woman and you want to marry her, invariably, almost without exception; there will be an enormous obstacle between you and the marrying of that woman that you will need to overcome that obstacle to marry her. I believe God and his providence allows these sorts of complications to conform us and press us into the image of Christ. Your character will be displayed through the heart attitude you have in meeting these obstacles.

There can be many obstacles or complications as a man pursues his Ruth. She may be a single mother. She may be a widow. She's still in college. She lives in another state. She's got a bunch of college debt. She's a little older and if you get married, she wants to start a family right away. She's a new Christian, she's going to need a lot of encouragement spiritually. Whatever it is, there will be an obstacle that you have to overcome.

I believe God brings obstacles for two reasons. One, it allows the man to settle the issue in his own heart, of how devoted he truly is to that woman. How much is he willing to sacrifice? What is he willing to work through? What is he willing to pay or endure to be with that woman? Secondly, it then reveals the depth of his commitment to the woman. She knows if he's willing to go through this, overcome that, work through this obstacle, overcome this financial difficulty or geographic limitation, he must really love me, because he is willing to go above and beyond the call of duty, because he so desperately wants to be with me.

The Providence of Authority

Ruth 4:1b | And behold, the redeemer, of whom Boaz had spoken, came by. So Boaz said, "Turn aside, friend; sit down here." And he turned aside and sat down.

Here is Boaz, a man of honor. He had all night with Ruth. He loves Ruth. That's precisely why he does not fornicate with her. He wants to do things morally, biblically, with dignity. He sits down at the gate, and as soon as he sits down, here what we read, "Behold," it just so happens, who comes by, Mr. What's-his-face. "The redeemer, of whom Boaz had spoken, came by." Here's again the providence of God, subtly working behind the scenes. Boaz was honorable with Ruth on the threshing floor, didn't have any inappropriate physical relations. Instead, he's trying to do things honorably, biblically, legally.

Mr. What's-his-face is a loser, because he is legally and spiritually obligated, as the closest living male relative to Naomi and Ruth, to take care of them. Deuteronomy 25 speaks of this. He needs to make sure they're prospering.

At this point, he has done nothing for these women; they're starving to death. He hasn't done anything. He probably lives a mile or two away. It's the little town of Bethlehem. This would be akin to, you being an adult male who owns your home and has a job, and your aunt, or your cousin lives a few miles away, and they're starving to death, and you don't even call. You don't check in. They're new to town. You don't even go visit. "How are you doing? Do you need any food? Your husbands are dead. Can I pray for you?" Nothing. This is a man who has abdicated all of his responsibilities. He has failed at them.

You might say, why are you being so hard on Mr. What's-His-Face? He hasn't done anything wrong. Actually, he has. There are sins of commission where you break God's law, and there are sins of omission where you neglect to do the good that you ought. James 4:17, "whoever knows the right thing to do and fails to do it, for him it is sin." This man neglected his own family. It was a small town. He didn't even know Naomi had a marriable daughter!

Mr. Nobody sins by omission, where he doesn't do anything. What was Adam's first sin? Eating the fruit? We could argue that. But I think his first sin was one of omission and neglect. Adam didn't say or do anything to protect his wife. And weak, cowardly, failed men don't do anything.

Naomi and Ruth are starving to death; they're at such a point of destitute poverty that Naomi is looking to sell the family land. Now, this is a big deal, because the land would have been passed on from one generation to the next. It was part of the legacy and lineage of the family. Of course, all of this works toward Boaz's favor. He loves Ruth, and the other man doesn't, and doesn't care at all about this part of his family. This is all part of God's providence. God is providing the circumstances for Boaz to legally marry Ruth.

The Plurality of Authority

Boaz gathers ten elders of the city for a legal transaction. He doesn't just consult with just one guy that's already on his side. He gets the impartial advice of a plurality of elders.

> **Ruth 4:2** | And he took ten men of the elders of the city and said, "Sit down here." So they sat down.

Boaz wants to marry Ruth. He doesn't just go out and marry her. Remember this is the time of the judges when "every man did that which was right in his own eyes." Boaz is rich and powerful. Yet he does not use bribes and his position to get his way. He does not believe himself to be above the law. He submits to his fellow brothers in the Lord. Boaz grabs ten guys who were elders and says, "I need to do a legal transaction. I need to do a business deal today. You, you, you, you, you, you sit down. We're going to do a legal transaction here. I need witnesses." He is leading the charge. He's doing it right. He's an honorable, godly businessman.

Boaz really wants to marry Ruth. There is a temptation to cut corners. There is a temptation not to submit to the wisdom of others. But he does succumb to that. Wherever you are there are always going to be things you don't agree with. There are always going to be things you wish you could do but you can't. That's life in submitting to authority. We all have to give an account to God, and we all have to have a good conscience.

There have been times in my life when I didn't agree with my authorities and mentors around me. That is always the case. We see things differently because we are made of sinful flesh. If everyone of course saw things my way the world would be a better place, right? No,

God puts godly authority in our lives to protects us. In this life you can always get what you want one way or another with enough excuses. Don't make excuses for disregarding authority. If you do that, God may take you out of the game for a season.

This is a good moment to emphasize the necessity of a plurality of elders in the local church. First, no one man is the fountain of perfect wisdom. A plurality of men will sharpen each other as iron sharpens iron. A group of men who are sincerely seeking after God brings a balance of wisdom. Second, no one man can lead an entire flock. Like Jesus, he has his closest inner circle of three. He has his twelve, but his influence after that is from a distance. There is also an accountability when there are many hearts of godly men overseeing the doctrine and practice of the church.

The Clarity of Authority

As we submit to authority, we will see that God can bring real clarity. It may not occur immediately. This is not microwave wisdom. As we wait on God to work through the godly men he's given to his people, we can expect God to give us clarity as to his will. We listen in on Boaz explaining his situation to the elders of Bethlehem. He addresses "Mr. So-and-So" first.

> **Ruth 4:3-4** | Then he said to the redeemer, "Naomi, who has come back from the country of Moab, is selling the parcel of land that belonged to our relative Elimelech. **4** So I thought I would tell you of it and say, 'Buy it in the presence of those sitting here and in the presence of the elders of my people.' If you will redeem it, redeem it. But if you will not, tell me, that I may know, for there is no one besides you to redeem it, and I come after you." And he said, "I will redeem it."

Here we see the motive of Mr. What's-His-Name. He gets to buy some cheap land. His motives are bad. Of course, he wants to redeem it. He doesn't know about Ruth. He doesn't know he'd have to raise up a family (Deut 25). He only thinks he can make a quick profit off of Naomi and Ruth's land.

Now, this man, Mr. Nobody, is a fool, because Boaz comes to him and says, "Do you want to buy some real estate?" And he basically says: "Yeah, I like real estate. Great." He doesn't get a contract. He doesn't survey the details. He doesn't look at the additional expenses.

Mr. Nobody hastily says in verse 4, "I will redeem it." At this point we are all saying: "Oh no! Stop the story! Don't let this Mr. Nobody take Ruth!" If the book of Ruth ended at Ruth 4:4, it would be a tragedy. Ruth can't marry this worthless Mr. Nobody. Yet, look at Boaz. He's not wringing his hands. He is a wise man meeting with other wise men. There is great safety in that. And just when we are about to give up and give in to Mr. So-and-So, Boaz steps in with the fine print. Now, Boaz, as a man of the word, knows exactly what he's doing here.

> **Ruth 4:5** | Then Boaz said, "The day you buy the field from the hand of Naomi, you also acquire Ruth the Moabite, the widow of the dead, in order to perpetuate the name of the dead in his inheritance."

Boaz says to the nearer kinsman, "You know, don't you, that Naomi has a daughter-in-law. So when you do the part of the kinsman redeemer, you must also take her as your wife and raise up offspring in the name of her husband Mahlon? Ruth is of child-rearing age, which means that if you bring her into your family then you have the responsibility to provide her with children, including an heir, a son who will then receive the inheritance of the land that you are purchasing."

Boaz, who has no legal obligation, is the only one who knows what's going on. He comes to this man and says, "Legally you have this opportunity to buy the land. The women are in dire circumstances. You need to make up your mind right now, do you want to buy the land or not? And if you don't want to buy it the land, I'll buy the land. I'll fix the mess. I'll take care of things. I'll do what's right."

> **Ruth 4:6** | Then the redeemer said, "I cannot redeem it for myself, lest I impair my own inheritance. Take my right of redemption yourself, for I cannot redeem it."

So all of a sudden this land that he's about to purchase that he had envisioned in his mind being passed down to his sons, now he's not going to get any of that. It's going to be passed down to this other son, by the way, a son born from marriage to Ruth the Moabitess. Mr. Nobody had to know the law in Deuteronomy 25.

> *Deuteronomy 25:5-6* | If brothers are living together and one of them dies without a son, his widow must not marry outside the family. Her husband's brother shall take her and marry her and fulfill the duty of a brother-in-law to her. The first son she bears shall carry on the name

of the dead brother so that his name will not be blotted out from Israel.

Boaz let's this man know the fine print. You've got to raise up babies for Ruth. "Do you like babies? Do you want some babies? A lot of men are like, "No. They're like sprinklers, fluids come out all the holes." Babies are a lot of work. More mouths to feed. More importantly, more hearts to train. Mr. Nobody has to walk away. (And everybody cheers)

CHECK YOUR MOTIVES (4:7-10)

Now we come to a place where Boaz has to check his motives. You have to realize he is committing to a woman with a lot of obstacles. She's older. She's been married for ten years. She's not had any children. Can he even raise up a seed for her? There are a lot of questions.

Motivated by Integrity

It becomes clear in verses 7 and following that Boaz has good motives for entering into this agreement. He has integrity. He's thought this through thoroughly. Mr. Nobody on the other hand, simply wants to pad his portfolio, but he's not able redeem Ruth, so he has to formally break his obligation to Ruth before the elders.

> **Ruth 4:7-8** | Now this was the custom in former times in Israel concerning redeeming and exchanging: to confirm a transaction, the one drew off his sandal and gave it to the other, and this was the manner of attesting in Israel. **⁸** So when the redeemer said to Boaz, "Buy it for yourself," he drew off his sandal.

A removed shoe was not like spitting in the face. It wasn't an insult. It was a picture that represented yielding the right to a property or the right to purchase that piece of land. This occurred regarding the property that belonged to Naomi and her family.

So, Mr. So-and-So takes his sandal off and gives it to Boaz. Boaz beaming from ear to ear receives the shoe. And then there is such joy – it's like in a Rocky movie when Rocky wins and the crowd just goes nuts erupting into applause. That's the picture here. "Buy it for yourself," and he gives the sandal to Boaz. This is the climax of the book of Ruth. It's like at the pinnacle of the movie when the crowd's is rejoicing. All the witnesses around are dancing in the streets, so to speak.

Motivated by Responsibility

Then Boaz calms the crowd down, orchestra music fades in the background into a nice soft lull for Boaz to give a final impassioned speech, his last words in the book. He's willing to take full responsibility for Ruth and Naomi and purchasing back all their properties. Listen to his speech.

> **Ruth 4:9-10** | Then Boaz said to the elders and all the people, "You are witnesses this day that I have bought from the hand of Naomi all that belonged to Elimelech and all that belonged to Chilion and to Mahlon. **10** Also Ruth the Moabite, the widow of Mahlon, I have bought to be my wife, to perpetuate the name of the dead in his inheritance, that the name of the dead may not be cut off from among his brothers and from the gate of his native place. You are witnesses this day."

For the first time the story refers explicitly to some land belonging to Elimelek, to his "share"—that is, his allocation within the land belonging to his clan. It is not clear what has happened to the land since Elimelek and his family left Judah for Moab some years ago, though we may guess that he had surrendered it as collateral or leased it to someone who had made a loan to him at the time of the famine. Apparently, it is then in some sort of limbo; its long-term destiny has not been sorted out, but anyone who wanted to take it over on a more permanent basis would have to "redeem" it—that is, pay Elimelech's debt.[38]

Boaz is at a station in life where he can actually afford to do this. This is one of the benefits of marrying an older, established man. He's been building his business. He's been making a living. He's been investing in real estate, and he's been investing wisely and tithing generously. And he has been conducting himself in a very responsible way, financially. A man first and foremost must love Jesus if he is going to marry my daughter. Secondly, he needs to be a responsible man with a job with benefits. Those two things are key!

Boaz wasn't worried about having the largest plasma TV on the block. He didn't care what level of the Mario Brothers or Donkey Kong video games he could get to. He was a man. Single men, if you are going to marry, you need to not only be a man, you need to live like a man

---

[38] Goldingay, *Ruth for Everyone*, 183.

and take responsibility. So we see when facing obstacles, we need to submit to authority, and we need to check our motives.

SEEK GOD IN PRAYER (4:11-12)

Finally, we need to seek God in prayer. Too many guys are chasing the pursuits of boys, rather than thinking, "How can this be an opportunity for me to grow spiritually, put to death sin, make some money, buy a house, learn some business skills, and invest in my future, so that if and when Ruth comes along, I'm ready to execute on the deal." The elders and the people begin to have a prayer meeting about this momentous transaction. How do they pray?

A Prayer for Legacy

First, the elders pray for a legacy for Boaz and Ruth. They know what God has done through Salmon and Rahab, Boaz's father and mother. Perhaps God will do more (and indeed he will). Listen to their prayer.

> **Ruth 4:11a** | Then all the people who were at the gate and the elders said, "We are witnesses. May the Lord make the woman, who is coming into your house, like Rachel and Leah, who together built up the house of Israel.

If we follow God with our whole heart, he can do infinitely more than our week flesh can do. Jesus said, "Without me you can do nothing" (Jn 15:5). Paul said, "In me, that is, in my flesh dwells no good thing" (Rom 7:14). Paul says to the Ephesians: I bow my knee to ask for the strength of the Spirit, the measureless love of Christ, and all the fullness of God. And if I ask for that, I can expect God to answer beyond my imagination.

> Ephesians 3:20–21 | Now to him who is able to do far more abundantly than all that we ask or think, according to the power at work within us, [21] to him be glory in the church and in Christ Jesus throughout all generations, forever and ever. Amen.

The people pray, "God, we pray that Ruth would be like the matriarchs Rachel and Leah, who were the mothers of the twelve tribes of Israel. Ruth has gone from the Moabite outsider to the highly respected matriarchal insider. The people now love her, and they have much hope for the children who will come from her. By the way, does God answer this prayer? Does Ruth become elevated to the level of Rachel and Leah? Yes!

A Prayer for Consistency

The elders continue to pray for Boaz, that he would be consistent and persevering in godliness. Remember this is the lawless time of the judges, so you can understand these godly men's excitement in this prayer.

> **Ruth 4:11b** | May you act worthily in Ephrathah and be renowned in Bethlehem.

What they're saying is this, "Boaz, you're a great man. We all know it. You're good in business. You love people. You're generous. You're kind. You bless everyone. Continue." Continue. Some men get off to a good start, and then get off track. You want to run your race well. You want to finish your life well, Paul says. They pray, Boaz, keep doing what you're doing. Don't mess this up.

A Prayer for Offspring

It's one thing to pray for a godly legacy, and for consistency, but now they pray for this holiness to be promoted through generations—to future children of Boaz and Ruth.

> **Ruth 4:12** | And may your house be like the house of Perez, whom Tamar bore to Judah, because of the offspring that the Lord will give you by this young woman."

Boaz and the Bethlehemites are descendants of Perez, so this is a great honor in this prayer. How long had she been married previously? Ten years. How many children did she have? Zero. What are they trusting God to do? Open her womb and enable her to become a mother. This is faith. They are asking for something that seems impossible. They are giving everything to the Lord. That was in the heart of Ruth. That was in the heart of Boaz. My question to you then is, are you living in such a way as to prepare yourself for marriage and family? Are you ready to form a legacy of godliness for the Lord?

Conclusion

Boaz shows us how our Kinsman-Redeemer, Jesus Christ, takes us as penniless foreigners and provides us with security, a future and a hope. Boaz is an amazing man, who has no legal obligation to do this.

It's just pure grace. Mr. What's-His-Face was legally obligated to do all of this. Boaz is doing it, not by obligation.

This union ultimately leads to the birth of a son; which eventually leads to the birth of whom? Jesus. Jesus is coming through this family. If it wasn't for Boaz you wouldn't get Jesus, that's how important it is that there's a good dad somewhere that makes a difference and a new family line.

6 | RUTH 4:13-22

TRUSTING GOD'S REDEEMER

Boaz took Ruth, and she became his wife. And he went in to her, and the Lord gave her conception, and she bore a son. Boaz fathered Obed, Obed fathered Jesse, and Jesse fathered David.
RUTH 4:13, 21-22

Every Christian is on earth to tell the story of Christ with his or her life. We go through trials and tribulations that seem to have no meaning. We are crucified with Christ. Our old life is dead. This life is painful and tedious at times. Yet like Christ we live the resurrected life. For the Christian death and pain and sorrow and tears are always swallowed up in victory.

So it is with Ruth. Ruth tells the story of the Christian life. The story of Ruth opens as bleak as can be. Three funerals leave Naomi and Ruth childless and penniless. Yet for Naomi and Ruth, there is a mighty resurrection of their lives as Boaz is set to marry Ruth. In all of Ruth and Naomi's struggles, they tell the story of Christ. Ruth tells the story of Christ in three ways. The marriage points to Christ (4:13a). The baby points to Christ (4:13b-17). The genealogy points to Christ (4:18-22).

THE MARRIAGE POINTS TO CHRIST (4:13A)

Ruth 4:13a | So Boaz took Ruth, and she became his wife.

Boaz marries Ruth. There is a wedding! Proverbs 4:12 says, "An excellent wife is the crown of her husband, but she who brings shame is like rottenness in his bones." Ruth is like a crown on Boaz's head, not a cancer. Ruth wasn't always a crown. She didn't start off as a crown. She started off as a Moabite worshiping Chemosh, probably immoral in her relationships, from a bad family in a horrible town. Her husband died. She was either barren, or she had offered her children in sacrifice to Chemosh. She's not a virgin, new to town, flat broke, and a new convert. But Ruth leaves all for the Lord. Of Ruth's sacrifice, the great Puritan Matthew Henry commented.

> The one that forsakes all for Christ shall find more than all with him; it shall be recompensed a hundredfold in this present time and much more in the life to come! [39]

Boaz and Ruth's marriage is a picture of Christ and his people (Eph 5:22-33). Boaz is a kinsman redeemer and is a type of Christ. Boaz is the foreshadowing of the ultimate redemption in Jesus. Ruth is the bride, foreshadowing of the church of Jesus Christ, Christ's bride. Let's draw some parallels so you understand the gospel out of the book of Ruth.

Jesus Became Our Near Kinsman

First, like Boaz, Jesus is our kinsmen redeemer. Boaz was a near kinsman to Ruth, and Jesus Christ, our glorious eternal God, became a man – entered into human history, took upon himself human flesh to identify with us to become our near kinsman. The apostle Paul describes it this way.

> *Philippians 2:6-8* | Though he was in the form of God, did not count equality with God a thing to be grasped, [7] but emptied himself, by taking the form of a servant, being born in the likeness of men. [8] And being found in human form, he humbled himself by becoming obedient to the point of death, even death on a cross.

---

[39] Matthew Henry, *Matthew Henry's Concise Commentary* (Oak Harbor, WA: Logos Research Systems, 1997), 257, comments on Ruth 4:13.

Jesus Paid the Price for His Bride

Boaz was able to redeem Ruth and pay off all her debts, and Jesus alone is able to redeem us from our sin debt. Boaz did it through financial wherewithal; Jesus did it through his sinless life to redeem our sinful life, and to give himself as the price for our redemption. Not only is he able to redeem us, but he is also like Boaz, *willing* to redeem us. Boaz was not forced or obligated to marry and redeem Ruth, and Jesus is not forced, or obligated to redeem us, but he is willing. Boaz did it out of love. Likewise, Jesus redeems out of love, and he's willing and able. He says, "Come to me, all who labor and are heavy laden, and I will give you rest" (Mt 11:28).

Boaz paid the full price to pay for Ruth's debt. Likewise, Jesus has paid the price for redemption. It cost Boaz a great deal to redeem Ruth, and it cost Jesus his own life. He went to the cross and died, to give himself, to pay the price for our sins, which is death. That's the penalty and price. And so, at the cross, Jesus was able and willing and did pay the price for our redemption. Likewise, the Lord Jesus redeems us, not by our participation, good works, morality, religion, purgatory, reincarnation, karma, none of those things. It's a gift. Boaz redeems Ruth. Boaz does all of the work. The Lord Jesus redeems us, his bride, the church, collectively, as a gift; he does all of the work. And Boaz takes Ruth to be his wife. He loves her, and he has an unbroken, ongoing relationship with her. So, Jesus Christ takes the church, his beloved bride, he loves her in an unbroken and unending continual relationship.

Like Ruth, we do nothing! As we read the story of Ruth and Boaz, and in this section, Ruth says and does nothing. Her redemption is a gift that is given to her; it is nothing that she participates in.

Jesus Completes the Work of Redemption

Finally, like Boaz, Jesus brings total redemption of his bride and the land. Boaz not only redeemed the woman, but he also redeemed the land. We're waiting for the Lord Jesus to return to finish and complete his work of redemption, and also to redeem the earth, which is his proverbial land. We take our cues as the church, the collective bride, from Ruth. She walked in holiness, and she trusted wholeheartedly. That's what we are to do by the grace that God gives us. We repent of sin and trust in our redeemer. We trust in his finished work, and we live the new life that he gives us. If you're not a Christian, you need to be redeemed like Ruth was.

We will one day rule and reign as God's kings and priests when our God and King, our great Boaz returns. Mortality will put on immortality. Corruption will put on incorruption. Death will be swallowed up in victory! God will wipe away all tears! What a wedding that will be! It will be the "marriage supper of the Lamb."

We are told there that one day we will hear the voice of a great multitude. A sea of people without number. It is the day when the trumpet sounds, and the dead in Christ rise. It will be the end of the ages. The Judgment Day. And the sheep will be gathered to Christ for a great wedding feast (*cf* Rev 19:6-9). Will you be there?

Are you looking forward to the heavenly marriage feast? Or are you living off of the maggot filled scraps that this life can offer you? Let's be feasting at the table of the King! Do you know Christ? Can you say, "I am his and he is mine?" (Song 2:16). Jesus is, in the words of Spurgeon, "Our glorious Boaz." He is our redeemer. He is a near kinsman.

THE BABY POINTS TO CHRIST (4:13B-17)

> **Ruth 4:13b** | And he went in to her, and the Lord gave her conception, and she bore a son.

The Baby's Mother is Redeemed

Here was a woman who had been married before for ten years and might have even offered a child to Chemosh but is now apparently barren. She comes to Israel with no children. God sometimes makes the barren woman to be "a joyful mother of children" (Psa 113:9). I want all of you ladies to understand, it really doesn't matter where you come from or what you've done, if you meet Jesus everything can and will change. You can have a horrible situation, make terrible choices as Ruth did, and you can have a wonderful conclusion, as Ruth does. The story opens with Ruth at a funeral as an unbelieving woman, and it concludes with her as a beloved, believing wife and mother who worships the God of the Bible, and that's a beautiful story of redemption. Ruth has gone from a foreigner (Ruth 1) to a servant of the Lord (Ruth 2) to a beautiful bride (Ruth 3-4).

We all like Ruth, though born in Moab, dead in sin, we have been born again from heaven by the Spirit. We are redeemed. Just like Ruth would never again be the godless Moabite that she was, so we can never be what we were before we knew Christ. We are crucified to sin and alive to God, instruments of righteousness and holiness.

The Baby's Parents are Chaste

I want you to notice a few things here. First, notice the short engagement. Short engagements are wise and good. This is probably the shortest engagement ever. The Scripture doesn't say, but it seems their engagement couldn't have been a week. Maybe it was a month. But it seems short! We encourage that at our local church. It is good to have a short engagement to encourage chastity in your singleness.

Notice that Boaz and Ruth are chaste until marriage, and then they make up for lost time. That's our position at our local church. Be chaste. Your future spouse is worth saving yourself. If you have failed, the blood of Jesus can cleanse you, but as a believer you want to remain chaste until marriage. You want to be a virgin. Boaz, as far as we know had never been married. They didn't listen to the lies of the world, like how do you know you love someone unless you sleep with them? I'll tell you what, they knew if they loved one another they wanted to give that which was most precious to each other on their wedding night, and not before.

Single people, you want your first romantic experience to be on your wedding night. Wait until the wedding night. You don't want to have to live with questions and comparisons in your life. You want to wait. You want to be chaste. So Boaz and Ruth are chaste before marriage, and then they made up for lost time! And they conceived!

The Baby's Birth is Miraculous

> **Ruth 4:13b** | And he went in to her, and the Lord gave her conception, and she bore a son.

Wow! A honeymoon baby! Ruth had been previously married for ten years. How many kids did she conceive? Likely zero. Ruth got married and conceived a child in the same day. God is so gracious! So the book of Ruth is surrounded by the grace of God. In chapter one, God gives a harvest after a long famine. In chapter 4, God gives a baby to a barren woman. God is good! "Every good and perfect gift comes from above, from the Father of lights" (Jas 1:17). And we serve that same God.

Some of our couples in our churches struggle with infertility. We are all for medical help if possible. We are all for adoptions. We as God's people ought to be those who love children whether we can have them or not. Perhaps God would burden some of you to adopt children. There are even times though it is not often, but at times God opens up the barren womb. He did that for Ruth. He does not do that for everyone.

The Bible says, "Children are a blessing from the Lord" (Psa 127:3). We live in a country that doesn't believe that. Children are a lot of work. They cost a lot of money. That's all true. But they are a blessing from the Lord. They are your legacy. Don't let the world's philosophy rob you of one of God's greatest blessings. The families of our country are having less and less children. It's sad. People are aborting God's greatest blessings. May God have mercy on our country. Listen, if you can have children, you ought to have as many as you possibly can and stay sane.

This baby was conceived by the will of God. Ruth couldn't conceive before, but now the baby engendered in Ruth's womb as an ancestor of King David and eventually to the Messiah, Jesus Christ, himself.

The Baby's Legacy is Renowned

So now the focus shifts to Ruth's mother-in-law, Naomi. And her friends and Bible study ladies come around her and pray over her.

> **Ruth 4:14** | Then the women said to Naomi, "Blessed be the Lord, who has not left you this day without a redeemer, and may his name be renowned in Israel!

There is a lot going on here. First, notice that this baby named Obed is called Naomi's redeemer. If you look at the structure of this sentence, it is saying that baby Obed is Naomi's redeemer.

Grandkids are like redemption. Grandkids make you happy. Grandkids are fun. Here is Naomi who has lost both of her sons. No mother ever expects to lose a child. It's brutal. God knows that. In Naomi's case, God gives Naomi a grandson, Obed, who is going to bring life into her life in a special way. Naomi's friends prophesy over Naomi.

> **Ruth 4:15** | He shall be to you a restorer of life and a nourisher of your old age, for your daughter-in-law who loves you, who is more to you than seven sons, has given birth to him.

My wife's folks actually got a bigger house when their children got married. I love it. You know why? For all the grandkids. Kids get married. Grandkids get married. Guess where our favorite place is? Grandma and Grandpa's! And my kids are a nourisher and restorer of life in their old age. Yes, grandkids bring great life. So the good life is not to have 20 girlfriends like Hollywood would like you to believe. The good life is to have lots of kids and lots of grandkids. That's the good life.

This baby's legacy is renowned, because eventually another baby would be born in Bethlehem, Jesus. All nations and families of the earth would be blessed through him. People from every tribe and tongue and people and nation will worship the Messiah.

The Baby's Influence is Multigenerational

Now notice in verse 16, Naomi has a very special relationship with her grandson, Obed. She becomes a mother to him.

> **Ruth 4:16** | Then Naomi took the child and laid him on her lap and became his nurse.

Naomi becomes a nursing mother to Obed. She raises him as if he were her own son. This is something Ruth did for Naomi, because she loved her mother-in-law so much. She knew she had two sons that died. She let her raise him it seems. It looks like she did a pretty good job because Obed's grandson was King David!

I want you to see this multi-generational godliness that is so lacking in our culture and even in our churches. The majority of us here are first generation Christians. Let us do all we can to stay close to one another as families. A child doesn't just need a mom and a dad. A child needs his or her grandparents. If you are godly, you ought to do all you can to be there for your kids and your grandkids. Look at Naomi.

Now in the church of God, we have a multi-generational family. In Christ, we are a body that is "fitly formed together in love" (Eph 4:15-16).

The Baby's Name Means "Worshipper"

> **Ruth 4:17** | And the women of the neighborhood gave him a name, saying, "A son has been born to Naomi." They named him Obed. He was the father of Jesse, the father of David.

Apparently, the women of the neighborhood in the little town of Bethlehem suggested the name that Naomi should suggest to Ruth. That name? It's very significant, like all the names in the book of Ruth. His name should be Obed, which means "worshipper."

That's how we ought to raise our children. We usually raise our voice in anger. We ought to raise our voice in worship. When is the last time you worshipped with your child? How about you Grandma and Grandpa – when is the last time you worshipped with the grandchildren. When did you get on your knees in worship and adoration with your children or grandchildren?

What a great name! It looks like Obed's life fits his name of "worshipper." He's going to learn to worship the Lord from Naomi and Ruth and Boaz and all the people of the neighborhood. That's a great environment to raise a child!

How appropriate that Obed's name means "worshipper" since many years from his birth, after the crucifixion and resurrection of Ruth's great, great, etc., grandson, Jesus Christ, there will be a pouring out of the Spirit on all flesh during the Harvest Festival where Ruth and Boaz got to know each other and eventually married. It is that Spirit that teaches us to worship God, in spirit and in truth.

THE GENEALOGY POINTS TO CHRIST (4:18-22)

Ruth 4:18-22 | Now these are the generations of Perez: Perez fathered Hezron, [19] Hezron fathered Ram, Ram fathered Amminadab, [20] Amminadab fathered Nahshon, Nahshon fathered Salmon, [21] Salmon fathered Boaz, Boaz fathered Obed, [22] Obed fathered Jesse, and Jesse fathered David.

Christ's Family is Divinely Constituted

Reading this genealogy is like reading the Hebrew phone book. Attached to each name is a story. Christ promises to build his church, and he says, "the gates of hell shall not prevail against it." There is no way such a group of people would ever gather on their own. God had to gather them and put them into the lineage of our Lord Jesus Christ. The Bible says that all God's people are "elect" and "chosen by God" (Eph 1:4). The people listed here would never have come to God. God has to draw us to himself (Jn 6:44).

God is telling us something here. He wants us to have something more than just a good time or a good weekend. He wants us to have a good legacy, and that legacy begins by following him. I'm so thankful God called me to himself when I was 15. I was on my way to destruction. My twin sister was the same way. By the time she was 20 she was on drugs, anorexic, and giving her body to a man that wasn't her husband. But Jesus changed us both. And now instead of going to rehab and having 20 girlfriends that can't read, I have a wife and five children, and God is giving us a good legacy. You don't want a good time. You want a good legacy! Receive the gift of eternal life and join in on this legacy.

Christ's Family is Diverse

The story of Ruth comes to an ultimate climax with the birth of Jesus (as Matthew's genealogy points out). It encourages readers to wonder how God's involvement in their everyday lives relates to a much bigger purpose of redemption.[40] The genealogy that caps off the book of Ruth (4:18-22) is almost identical to Matthew.

> *Matthew 1:1-6* | The book of the genealogy of Jesus Christ, the son of David, the son of Abraham. ²Abraham was the father of Isaac, and Isaac the father of Jacob, and Jacob the father of Judah and his brothers, ³and Judah the father of Perez and Zerah by Tamar, and Perez the father of Hezron, and Hezron the father of Ram, ⁴and Ram the father of Amminadab, and Amminadab the father of Nahshon, and Nahshon the father of Salmon, ⁵and Salmon the father of Boaz by Rahab, and Boaz the father of Obed by Ruth, and Obed the father of Jesse, ⁶and Jesse the father of David the king. And David was the father of Solomon by the wife of Uriah.

Listed are four Canaanite women are mentioned here in Matthew. Look at this genealogy. This redeemer Obed points to Christ and his church! Perez came from Tamar, and according to Philo, a Jewish historian, Tamar was likely a Gentile – a Canaanite.[41] Salmon was married to Rahab, a Canaanite from Jericho. Boaz is married to Ruth the Moabite. Remember King David's son Solomon is born to Bathsheba, who

---

[40] Goldingay, *Ruth for Everyone*, 187–188.
[41] Philo, a Jewish exegete who lived at the time of Matthew, wrote this about her: "Tamar was a woman from Syria Palestina who had been bred up in her own native city, which was devoted to the worship of many gods, being full of statues, and images, and, in short, of idols of every kind and description. But when she, emerging, as it were, out of profound darkness, was able to see a slight beam of truth, she then, at the risk of her life, exerted all her energies to arrive at piety…living for the service of and in constant supplication to the one true God" (*Virt.* 220–22).

is married to Uriah the Hittite. Most Bible scholars believe Bathsheba herself was also a Hittite woman. Look at all these Gentile women in the line of our Savior! All four women are mentioned in Matthew's genealogy of Jesus! What we have is a preview of the church of Jesus Christ. This royal line of Jesus points to a church that includes "every tribe, tongue, people, and nation" who will shout praises to the Lord. He is worthy!

Consider this as well: Tamar and Rahab were harlots. We know about the sin of David and Bathsheba. Ruth before she was a believer worshipped Chemosh. She and her sister Orpah were likely the daughters of Eglon, king of the Moabites. Jesus' family is filled with sinners because that's the only kind of people Jesus saves. Remember the words of Jesus, "Those who are well have no need of a physician, but those who are sick. 32 I have not come to call the righteous but sinners to repentance" (Lk 5:31-32). Ruth was from Moab, and Christ's family is "from every nation under heaven" (Acts 2:5; *cf* Rev 7:9).

Christ's Family is Delivered

The close of the book points to its theological significance by linking Ruth's story to David's and ultimately to our deliverance from sin, death, and hell through Jesus Christ. Until this closing paragraph, you might think you are simply reading a short story about some ordinary people's ordinary lives and the way God is involved in them. But it is typical of biblical stories about ordinary individuals to show how they relate to God's wider and longer purpose of redeeming the world through David's greater Son, Jesus Christ.

Ultimately, the book of Ruth leads to the cross. Ruth progenerates the line of the Savior. It is through this child's bloodline that all the nations of the world will be blessed. It's not exclusively a Jewish bloodline. It is a bloodline that includes Jews and Gentiles. And so we get a picture of heaven. Heaven is a place where we see "every tribe, tongue, people, and nation" worshipping the Lamb. We want our church to look like heaven!

Pills, and books, and a great job, and relationships and seminars – that can't make you happy. What makes us happy? The scarlet thread of the Bible, the thread of *redemption* in Christ will truly satisfy us. Christ satisfies. He heals. What is in common with all these names? They are the family of Jesus Christ. Jesus calls all to come to him.

What are Ruth and Naomi without a Redeemer? They are penniless. Barren. Homeless. No legacy. No hope. But Boaz comes along, and there is Ruth. She goes from penniless to provided for. She goes from barren to a bountiful mother in the genealogy of Christ. She goes from forgotten to favored, loved, and cherished.

Conclusion

Ruth and Boaz, and Naomi – their lives all point to Christ. The marriage, the baby, the genealogy. It all points to Christ. They lived for the coming redeemer. How about your life? Does it point to Christ?

I would be remiss not to end the book of Ruth with a call for you to come to the Redeemer. I had urged my twin sister Tammie, to go to a gospel preaching church service and consider the gospel. I had prayed for her for ten years. She had heard the truth that Christ died for her sins many times. It never hit home until one day in March of 1999. There was a church of 25 people meeting in a garage 50 feet from our childhood home in the bayou of Louisiana. This is a mile in the woods. The message was given. Christ Jesus died for sinners. She said, "I don't think God can love me. I'm too bad to be saved." This little twelve-year-old girl told her: "That's just who Jesus saves. You can only come to Jesus if you feel like you are unworthy and in need of the Savior." That day my sweet sister was born again! She was redeemed!

It wasn't my sister's pills that saved her. It wasn't any relationship that rescued her. It was Christ! It is Christ alone that can help us! He suffered, bled, and died to redeem you from your sins. He will make you clean. He will remove the stains of your sin. Come to Jesus!

7 | IMAGES OF THE SPIRIT IN RUTH

And at mealtime Boaz said to her, "Come here and eat some bread and dip your morsel in the wine." So she sat beside the reapers, and he passed to her roasted grain. And she ate until she was satisfied, and she had some left over.
RUTH 2:14

Why have a closing chapter on the Spirit of God in the book of Ruth when the Holy Spirit is never mentioned in the story? We will find that so much that is in the book of Ruth points to the ministry of the Holy Spirit, though the Spirit of God is never named in its pages.

The book of Ruth has been traditionally read every year on the day of Pentecost by the people of Israel, even to this day. Of all the five scrolls read at feasts throughout the Jewish year—the favorite of many is the book of Ruth. In the Old Testament, Pentecost is called the Feast of Weeks, the harvest festival that falls fifty days after the Feast of Firstfruits. Traditionally, Pentecost is also the feast that commemorates that earthshaking day when God gave the Law to Israel on Mount Sinai, the day when the congregation of God's people made a commitment: "We will do everything the Lord has said to do" (Exo 19:8). The rabbis saw it as Israel's betrothal to her God. As we read Ruth, we look forward to the time when the Mosaic law is utterly done away with because a new and higher law has replaced it, the law of the Spirit of life. The pictures of the Spirit in the book of Ruth, many feel, are irresistible. Ruth marries Boaz. The nation of Israel marries God. She's a Gentile, yet she's in the line of Jesus! It's a story of a commitment to God, an abundant harvest, and a marriage. There is unspeakable joy. It all points us to the outpouring of the Spirit at Pentecost.

The Feast of Weeks is best known in the New Testament as Pentecost. Jews from around the empire were gathered in Jerusalem one Pentecost long ago, and the Spirit of God fell on a group of believers gathered to worship and wait for the Messiah. The good news these believers proclaimed in various languages would mark the beginning of a vast and rapid expansion of God's people that would include Gentiles as well as Jews. So much that is in the book of Ruth points to the ministry of the Holy Spirit, though the Spirit of God is never named in its pages.

THE SPIRIT AND A FOREVER FAMILY

Ruth 1:16-17 | Ruth said, "Do not urge me to leave you or to return from following you. For where you go I will go, and where you lodge I will lodge. Your people shall be my people, and your God my God. **17** Where you die I will die, and there will I be buried. May the Lord do so to me and more also if anything but death parts me from you."

Ruth came from a place of paganism as a widow. No husband. No children. No legacy. She goes to a new place, with new faith, trusting in the Lord, and what does she do? She marries into the family of God. In Ruth, God is creating a picture over the centuries to represent his ultimate plan for the nations. He would bring a multi-ethnic harvest into his inheritance through a romantic redemption. Ruth pictures the story of us all. We were all born in Moab, dead in trespasses and sin (Eph 2:1-3). But God, rich in mercy, called us to himself, and gave us a new life, a new inheritance, and a family through his Redeemer, our glorious Boaz named Jesus Christ.

Just as Ruth was grafted into the people of God, so we are grafted into Christ and the Holy Spirit seals this union by permanently indwelling every believer. While the child of God may sin and grieve the Spirit, the Spirit will never leave the true believer. Absence of the Holy Spirit is the mark of the unsaved. The indwelling Holy Spirit is the seal of God's ownership upon the believer's heart. This ministry guarantees the security of the believer "until the day of redemption" (Eph 4:30). The Holy Spirit doesn't just seal us, but he sovereignly bestows spiritual gifts or abilities for service in the church to every believer (1 Pet 4:10; 1 Cor 12:7). It is through the gifts given to the believer that Christ does his work in and through his body in the areas of evangelism and Christian growth.

THE SPIRIT AND THE HARVEST

First, we see that Naomi and Ruth are leaving Moab and have hope for the harvest in Israel.

> **Ruth 1:22** | So Naomi returned, and Ruth the Moabite her daughter-in-law with her, who returned from the country of Moab. And they came to Bethlehem at the beginning of barley harvest.

Then we see the celebration of the harvest with Boaz and Ruth.

> **Ruth 2:14-15** | And at mealtime Boaz said to her, "Come here and eat some bread and dip your morsel in the wine." So she sat beside the reapers, and he passed to her roasted grain. And she ate until she was satisfied, and she had some left over. ¹⁵ When she rose to glean, Boaz instructed his young men, saying, "Let her glean even among the sheaves, and do not reproach her. ¹⁶ And also pull out some from the bundles for her and leave it for her to glean, and do not rebuke her."

It's no coincidence that the Spirit came at a harvest festival called the "Feast of Weeks," and it's fitting that the book Jews still read today at that festival is Ruth—a story of an impoverished Gentile who became one of God's people by marriage to a man with an inheritance in the land.

In the spirit of the harvest and God's love reaching all peoples and nations, the Jewish nation read the book of Ruth in its entirety at Pentecost. It is perfect for the season in that it speaks of famine and God restoring the harvest in Bethlehem (the breadbasket of Israel) Bethlehem literally means "House of Bread." How wonderful that Jesus, the true bread which comes down from heaven was born there. How wonderful that he came to save the last, the least, and the lost and that his lineage is drawn directly from the book of Ruth. How incredible that Jesus is descended from Ruth, a woman of Moab. What a glorious picture of God's love extending to those who have nothing, even to the nations. For it is not our righteousness that saves us. It is not our heritage that saves us. It is not our wealth that saves us. It is the gracious love of God in Jesus that feeds us, sustains us, and gives us eternal life.

Somewhere around A.D. 30, the fruit of an even greater harvest issued forth, for it was on the first day after the Sabbath that occurred in the midst of the Passover celebration that Jesus rose from the dead (Mt 28:1–10). Lest there be any doubt that his resurrection fulfilled the Feast of Firstfruits, Paul tells us explicitly that Christ is the firstfruits of those who will be raised from the dead (1 Cor 15:20–23). Just as the firstfruits offered to God under the old covenant anticipated the fuller harvest to come, the resurrection of Jesus anticipates the bodily resurrection of his people first promised under the old covenant (Job 19:25–27).

Fifty days after the Feast of Firstfruits was the Feast of Weeks, or Pentecost (from the Greek term *pentekostos*, or fiftieth), which was the grand celebration at the end of the grain harvest when the book of Ruth was traditionally read. On this occasion, the offerings of food and animals to the Lord were more lavish (Lev 23:15–22), an appropriate way to thank him for the tremendous bounty he had provided.

Just as Ruth celebrated the harvest and gathered her barley for her and Naomi to overflow and abundance, the Spirit of God has an overflowing harvest for us. The Holy Spirit is the agent of salvation who draws us to the love of Christ. The Spirit opens our eyes to see Christ and brings conviction to us so that we might clearly see the truth of the gospel in a clear light. It is God's Holy Spirit who grants us repentant faith. All who respond to this conviction and place their faith in Jesus Christ are born again and have a new nature. The Holy Spirit unites the believer with Christ and places him in the body of Christ, the church. He also unites the believer with Christ in his death, enabling him to live victoriously over sin. The Holy Spirit controls the believer who yields to God and submits himself to God's word. When these conditions are met, the believer lives in the power of the Spirit and produces the fruit of the Spirit which is the true harvest that God delights in.

THE SPIRIT AND FAITH

Ruth 3:6-9 | So she went down to the threshing floor and did just as her mother-in-law had commanded her. ⁷And when Boaz had eaten and drunk, and his heart was merry, he went to lie down at the end of the heap of grain. Then she came softly and uncovered his feet and lay down. ⁸ At midnight the man was startled and turned over, and behold, a woman lay at his feet! ⁹ He said, "Who are you?" And she answered, "I am Ruth, your servant. Spread your wings over your servant, for you are a redeemer."

Ruth had the faith to follow the wisdom of her mother-in-law Naomi to go and meet Boaz, and in faith propose that he propose for marriage!

In Christ, we are called to follow the wisdom, first and foremost, of the word of God, as well as the Spirit, and godly people within his church. There are many "Naomis" in our life that are willing to guide us. Indeed, we cannot live the Christian life alone, but we must be "fitly joined together" as we "build each other up in love" (Eph 4:15-16).

THE SPIRIT AND THE GENTILES

Ruth 4:5 | Then Boaz said, "The day you buy the field from the hand of Naomi, you also acquire Ruth the Moabite, the widow of the dead, in order to perpetuate the name of the dead in his inheritance."

From the first to the last chapter in Ruth, we are all very aware that she is a Moabite, a Gentile, i.e. a non-Jew from a non-believing nation. Even from the beginning of Abraham's story and the promise God gave him, God's chosen people were to be a light to the nations.

Genesis 12:2-3 | I will make of you a great nation, and I will bless you and make your name great, so that you will be a blessing. ³ I will bless those who bless you, and him who dishonors you I will curse, and in you all the families of the earth shall be blessed.

Galatians 3:8-9 | The Scripture, foreseeing that God would justify the Gentiles by faith, preached the gospel beforehand to Abraham, saying, "In you shall all the nations be blessed." ⁹ So then, those who are of faith are blessed along with Abraham, the man of faith.

Throughout scripture, God-fearing people everywhere were drawn to Israel's faith. There were Egyptians who left with Israel in the Exodus, a harlot of Jericho who joined God's people in the conquest of Canaan, Gentiles who served God during the ministries of Elijah and Elisha, a queen who came to Jerusalem to marvel at Solomon's wisdom and wealth, Assyrians who repented at Jonah's preaching, and Romans who aligned themselves with Jewish synagogues. The international, multi-ethnic, multi-lingual message of God's kingdom was not a New Testament innovation. God has always been relentless about drawing the world to himself.

God calls and equips his people to be fruitful. Jesus made that clear through numerous parables and principles. His kingdom is in a long harvest season of gathering sheaves of grain from the fields. Like Ruth, we're invited into his fields to work. He makes sure we're protected from those who would harm us or send us away, and he leaves plenty of gleanings so we can gather with him.

THE SPIRIT AND INHERITANCE

> **Ruth 4:9-10** | Boaz said to the elders and all the people, "You are witnesses this day that I have bought from the hand of Naomi all that belonged to Elimelech and all that belonged to Chilion and to Mahlon. ¹⁰ Also Ruth the Moabite, the widow of Mahlon, I have bought to be my wife, to perpetuate the name of the dead in his inheritance, that the name of the dead may not be cut off from among his brothers and from the gate of his native place. You are witnesses this day."

The overall story is that of Naomi and how she has lost her inheritance during a famine in Israel. She now has one of her daughters-in-law, Ruth that has joined her, so the situation is even more dire. Without an inheritance they will live in poverty and die without any heir or legacy.

This was our situation before we came to know Christ. We were heirs of the lake of fire, destined to eternal poverty. We had forfeited any heavenly inheritance through our sin in Adam. Through Christ, we regain our inheritance in the new birth, which is God himself.

> *1 Peter 1:4* | Born again... to an inheritance that is imperishable, undefiled, and unfading, kept in heaven for you.

What is this inheritance? Our inheritance is not merely the streets of gold, the crowns of glory, or the celestial cities. Oh yes, we get all that. But that is like the wrapping on the candy bar. Our inheritance is God. It is communion with Him forever and ever. We are heirs of God and joint heirs with Christ. What did Christ have before the worlds were created? He had the Father. The Father and the Son and the Spirit is our inheritance. Remember what God told Abraham? Genesis 15:1,

"The word of the LORD came unto Abram in a vision, saying, Fear not, Abram: I am your shield, and your exceeding great reward." What is our reward in paradise, in heaven? We get God as our inheritance!

THE SPIRIT AND THE BRIDE

Ruth 4:13a | So Boaz took Ruth, and she became his wife.

Ruth's story is a story of marriage, and the romance begins with Boaz drawing Ruth to himself, just as the Spirit draws us to God. Boaz gave Ruth such a big meal with extra to bring to Naomi. Isn't it wonderful how the Spirit wooed us before we belonged to him? He showed us how God would love us and care for us even before we trusted in him. Boaz is a marvelous picture of the Spirit's wooing.

Ruth's marriage propels forward with a proposal that Boaz propose. There is a seeking after Boaz. And God said, "You shall find me if you seek after me with all your heart." This is what Ruth did, and she beautifully pictures the seeking sinner coming to Christ, powerless, possessing nothing but faith alone in Christ alone.

Ruth's romance with Boaz represents everything a marriage is meant to be: holy, heaven-sent, and heartwarming. It's a picture, Paul says, of our relationship with Christ (Eph 5:22-33).

God's ultimate purpose for his people is like Boaz' ultimate purpose for Ruth: marriage and children. We see that at a great wedding at the end of Revelation. One gets the impression that God orchestrated the remarkable events of Ruth all along—across cultures, geographical boundaries, and adverse circumstances—in order to bring Boaz and Ruth together as a match made in heaven. And one gets the impression from the Bible as a whole that he's been doing the same in bringing us to Jesus. Scripture is clear that God is preparing a bride for his Son; this is what all of history is leading up to. Like Ruth, the bride of Christ begins as a foreigner from an immoral land steeped in idolatry; but in our desolation, we commit to him and he takes us in. We go from forsaken widow to beloved bride, and the blessings of the kingdom are ours to enjoy.

The book of Ruth is a romance with a very happy ending—just as scripture is as a whole. It's a cosmic story played out on a very personal scale in a seemingly random story in the Old Testament. Ultimately, the book of Ruth is our story too. It's the story of any human being who leaves everything behind to believe in Israel's God and the Redeemer he has provided. That's a choice that is filled with blessing and grafts us forever into the family of God.

THE SPIRIT AND THE BABY

> **Ruth 4:13-14** | So Boaz took Ruth, and she became his wife. And he went in to her, and the Lord gave her conception, and she bore a son. **14** Then the women said to Naomi, "Blessed be the Lord, who has not left you this day without a redeemer, and may his name be renowned in Israel!

Now the baby that is born is a special baby. He is in the line of the Messiah. His mother is a Gentile, and his father is half-Gentile. And that baby is the product of the grace of God, for his grandmother was a Gentile prostitute from Jericho named Rahab. God can do marvelous things to cleanse our past and make us a new creation.

We are called, like Ruth and Boaz to reproduce. They reproduced physically, and their seed was in the line of the Messiah. We as New Testament Christians are to reproduce by making disciples. What love they had for each other, and the fruit of their love was children. So it is with the believer. The fruit of our relationship with God is spiritual children. We are called not only to be children of God and *be disciples* of Christ, but we are also called to *make disciples* of all nations. We are to birth spiritual children constantly in our walk with the Lord.

THE SPIRIT AND WORSHIP

> **Ruth 4:17** | And the women of the neighborhood gave him a name, saying, "A son has been born to Naomi." They named him Obed. He was the father of Jesse, the father of David.

The climax of the story of Ruth is the baby that is born. His name is Obed, which means "worshipper." Isn't this another picture of the Spirit of God? He makes all who are born of him worshippers of the truth and living God. God is Spirit, and they who worship him must worship him in spirit and in truth.

Conclusion

Whether it is Pentecost Sunday or any Lord's Day, I want you to imagine you are on the southern steps of the Temple in Jerusalem where Peter was. He spoke to anywhere between thirty and sixty thousand people at that time. Jesus is proclaimed. Tongues of fire are resting above the heads of the disciples. The waters of baptism are stirring there, where there are still ritual baths there today with flowing water from underground springs.

Will you remember all that you have in the Spirit of God today? Ruth had so much, but she was just the black and white picture. You have the fullness of the Spirit. Won't you enjoy God's full inheritance for you by yielding completely and wholeheartedly to the Spirit? Amen!

You may obtain this and many other fine resources made available by Proclaim Publishers by contacting us:

Web:
proclaimpublishers.com

Email:
contact@proclaimpublishers.com

Postal Mail:
Proclaim Publishers
PO Box 2082
Wenatchee, WA 98807

Soli Deo Gloria

www.ingramcontent.com/pod-product-compliance
Lightning Source LLC
Chambersburg PA
CBHW031452040426
42444CB00007B/1069